Academic Programming
at CHICON IV

PATTERNS OF THE FANTASTIC

Edited by
Donald M. Hassler

BORGO PRESS / WILDSIDE PRESS

www.wildsidepress.com

This book is dedicated to my mother,
Frances Parsons Hassler

copyright © 1983 by Starmont House, P.O. Box 851, Mercer Island, Washington

Library of Congress Cataloging in-Publication Data

Chicon (4th : 1982 : Chicago, Ill.)
   Patterns of the fantastic.

   (Starmont studies in literary criticism, ISSN 0737-1306 ; no. 1)
   Reprint. Originally published: Mercer Island, Wash. Starmont House, 1983.
   Includes bibliographical references.
   1. Science fiction—Congresses. I. Hassler, Donald II. Title. III. Series.
[PN3433.2.C64 1982a]   809.3'876   83-12225
ISBN 0-89370-738-4 (PBK)
ISBN 0-916732-62-2

Contents

Preface

Introduction: Science Fiction and Fantasy
    and the Academic Enterprise
        Donald M. Hassler   1

Stephen King in Context
        Joseph F. Patrouch, Jr.   5

Science Fiction Women: Victims, Rebels, Heroes
        Richard Law   11

The Woman Science Fiction Writer and the
    Non-Heroic Male Protagonist
        Jim Villani   21

The Days of Future Past or Utopians Lessing and
    LeGuin Fight Future Nostalgia
        Kathe Davis Finney   31

Narcissism and Romance in McCaffrey's *Restoree*
        Mary T. Brizzi   41

Woman on the Edge of Narrative: Language in
    Marge Piercy's Utopia
        David L. Foster   47

The Metalinguistic Racial Grammar of Bellona:
    Ethnicity, Language and Meaning in
    Samuel R. Delany's *Dhalgren*
        Marleen Barr   57

Harlan Ellison's Use of the Narrator's Voice
        Joseph F. Patrouch, Jr.   63

The Social Science Fiction of Robin Cook
        Thom Dunn   67

Moon-Watcher, Man, and Star-Child:
    2001 as Paradigm
        Richard D. Erlich   73

Science Fiction Theater the Moebius Way
        Jane Bloomquist and William McMillan   81

Freaking the Mundane: A Sociological Look at
    Science Fiction Conventions, and Vice Versa
        Phyllis J. Day and Nora G. Day   91

Appendix: Academic Program at Chicon IV   103

Preface

In a dark economy and in the shadow of eternal mutability such as the loss of Philip K. Dick, 1982 was nevertheless a great year for science fiction and fantasy. Major new books from Asimov, Clarke, Heinlein, and Hubbard were balanced by exciting work from newer writers. Scholarly conferences and published work by commentators on the genre continued to grow, and the 40th World Science Fiction Convention initiated an academic programming track that was the seedbed for this book. It is appropriate that Starmont House, under the direction of T. E. Dikty, should publish <u>Patterns of the Fantastic</u> since the husband and wife team of Dikty and Julian May, herself an important novelist, suggested and encouraged all along the way this venture of academics at Chicon IV. What follows is a mix of work from historians, critics, sociologists, writers; and some variations in the approach to text and documentation reflect these different academic disciplines. Also, a number of papers and discussions were included in the program that could not be collected here. The entire program as it took place in Chicago is listed in the appendix.

In addition to the Diktys, many people helped in the organization of the academic programming at Chicon IV and in the preparation of this book. Carl Yoke gave me early advice. My wife, Sue Hassler, was my continual companion and assistant at the convention. The Chicon IV Program Division, under the leadership of Yale Edeiken and Greg Bennett, sponsored our program and looked after us. The officers of the Science Fiction Research Association encouraged and supported this new approach to the study of the genre, and the Kent State University Research Council supported the typing of the book manuscript and some of my travel. Barbara Burner, again, typed carefully and well from a difficult manuscript.

D.M.H.
January 1, 1983

Donald M. Hassler

Introduction: Science Fiction and Fantasy and the Academic Enterprise

Although it was not planned this way, the papers from the academic programming track that were submitted for publication and ultimately selected for this collection contain a persistent theme and, finally, a unity that I had not totally understood upon first hearing them and then selecting them for this book. The academic enterprise, though graced with quantum leaps now and then, can grow in a conversational way so that the more ideas are ruminated, perhaps, the clearer they become. In the fall of 1982, many of us seemed to have reflected on similar ideas. Those ideas have to do with the discernment of patterns of identity, including the identity of the academic enterprise itself, with the ways in which narrative patterns capture identity patterns, with teleology almost in an Aristotelian sense, with outcast individuals and outcast groups as special avenues to understanding our telos, and most generally, as with all questions Aristotelian, with matters of belief.[1] This short introductory essay will reflect a little further on these ideas and these unities in order to prepare the way for the papers themselves.

I need to acknowledge at the outset, however, two strong caveats against the paradoxically serendipitous and teleological patterning that I intend to suggest here. Both these caveats were part of the original and actual conversation of the academic track in Chicago though the second, as I will show, has most recently appeared in a published form that indicates a longer rumination of it by its author throughout the spring and summer of 1982. The first two sessions on Friday afternoon of the academic track addressed theoretical issues in the study of science fiction and fantasy; and as the schedule printed in the appendix to this book suggests, provocative statements on the nature of our enterprise were presented by former presidents of the Science Fiction Research Association: Thomas D. Clareson, James Gunn, and Arthur O. Lewis, Jr. Sandwiched among his three

fellow presidents, moreover, Joe De Bolt presented the most
provocative statement and the strongest caveat for this book
-- the warning of a sociologist against the impressionistic
tactics of his less scientific colleagues. De Bolt urged
that systematic patterns of investigation be used to supplement
literary interpretation of texts. He implied, in fact, that
the academic enterprise dealing with science fiction and fantasy
was haphazard, overly burdened with the ego of the investigator,
and generally non-systematic.

Following the session in which De Bolt asked for a different
kind of discipline in our studies of science fiction and fantasy,
Orson Scott Card read a paper that had just appeared in print
in which he countered that the critic, rather than being a
scientist, is actually a teller of tales about tales.[2] Card's
ideas coincide with my own notions of a teleology deriving
from narrative that will become apparent later in this
introductory essay and that will be exemplified in the papers
themselves. Significantly, the concluding paper in this book
written by sociologists goes beyond the data collected to
matters of belief, but first the second caveat.

Algis Budrys also spoke in the second session on Friday
afternoon. And his pair of caveats against the telos that
the academic enterprise hopes for must be acknowledged because
Budrys is a fine writer and ultimately, I think, dismissed
because Budrys is "telling the story" of fallibility that
only confirms the academic enterprise as a human enterprise,
with all the possibilities for transcendence that go with our
humanness. I have a long personal letter from Budrys with an
outline, which he spoke from in part during his session of the
academic track; and the reader can study at leisure the Budrys
attack on the academic enterprise in the January 1983 issue of
Fantasy and Science Fiction, which must have been written about
the time of his letter to me in late spring 1982.[3] From his
long experience in the field and wide knowledge, Budrys is
able to develop a convincing analysis of the affects of
marketing labels and other aspects of 20th-century publishing
on the literature itself; and I am sure he will eventually
complete this analysis.[4] His major caveat, however, seems to
be that the academic enterprise dealing with science fiction
and fantasy is self-serving and riddled with error.

I would offer the following papers, some of which Budrys
may have heard read, as examples of attempts to see patterns
of meaning in small segments of the larger pattern that we
call science fiction and fantasy. The authors of the papers
are driven by strong commitments grounded, I assume, in their
own self-understandings and interests; and the papers may now
and then contain error. But, in the acts of reading and
publishing their papers, the authors invite the correction of
error as well as the continuing conversation about the patterns
of meaning. I should think Budrys would not be upset as this
human dialogue continues -- unless his standards and expectations
are somehow more than human. It seems, finally, that both
De Bolt and Budrys call for more "facts" and less "story."
But if there is one telos that literature teaches us, it is
that the facts of human significance are better revealed in
narrative than in any other form.

As I implied to begin with, it is uncanny how uniform the
narrative patterns are in the papers that follow. To begin

at the end, perhaps, Phyllis and Nora Day argue that fandom itself is grounded on something resembling religious faith and populated with a particularly candid and attractive variety of outcasts, who are both hopeful and concerned about changing things for the better in the ghastly, nearly unreal world of the 20th century. If that is not a narrative scenario for a classic telos with echoes of Prometheus, an alienated Superman from a distant planet, and Wonder Woman as feminist champion, sociologists do not write questionnaires. The story is retold, more or less, by each of the writers treated in this book. Prometheus is usually woman, or black, or outcast of some sort; and the teleology that is searched for in the narrative patterns is a revolutionary teleology of how things might be rather than how they are.

Even though in several instances telos itself is debunked (as in Kathe Finney's paper especially but also, to some extent, in the papers by Richard Law and Jim Villani), the pattern is the familiar "demything" that intends to substitute the better pattern, story or myth. What is never forgotten or rejected in the telling of each of these stories about stories is the significance of the telos of narrative itself. The academic enterprise as represented by the authors of the papers in this book has strangely turned to science fiction and fantasy as a literature in which significant beliefs can be rediscovered. This is not a "metafiction" presented in these papers concerned only with itself as literature. For example, both David Foster and Marleen Barr point to the role of women and racial minorities in their writers respectively as the possible cutting edge of a new and needed social order. And the evolution that they envision is not just random but teleological.

Nearly all of the authors of the papers in this book are also conscious of evolution in the academic enterprise itself. They know that science fiction and fantasy as a popular literature is unusual to study and that their studies may be at the cutting edge of change in academe. For example, Thom Dunn insists on writing on a "merely" popular writer and, also, insists on using the feminine third-person. Richard Erlich's paper militantly places nearly as many words in the notes as in the body, indicating how change toward the future borrows from the past at times; and I have not edited him into conformity with current academic decorum. Jane Bloomquist and William McMillan write on improvisational theatre inspired by science fiction and fantasy, and Joseph Patrouch writes in part on a return to oral traditions in narrative. These patterns are not complete, of course; but they all share a seriousness about meaning that is their unifying pattern. The fairy tales that are evoked by Mary Brizzi, no more nor less than all of the narratives studied here, are stories that use elements of the fantastic to point the reader toward a definite end.

Kent State University

Notes

[1] Another serendipity this fall has been my reading of Alasdair MacIntyre, After Virtue: A Study of Moral Theory (Notre Dame: Univ. of Notre Dame, 1981), as well as John

Gardner's last novel <u>Mickelsson's Ghosts</u> (New York: Knopf, 1982). These two books have influenced this introductory essay.

[2] The essay has appeared in <u>The Science Fiction Review</u> edited by Richard Geis, but I have only seen it in manuscript and heard it read.

[3] The Algis Budrys letter to me is dated May 17, 1982. His essay is in his regular review column in <u>Fantasy and Science Fiction</u>, 64:1 (January 1983), 19-27.

[4] See the fine essay by Budrys on this topic entitled "Fiction in the Chain Mode: Nonliterary Influences on Science Fiction," <u>Science Fiction Dialogues</u>, ed. Gary Wolfe (Chicago: Academy, 1982), pp. 58-70.

Joseph F. Patrouch, Jr.

Stephen King in Context

　　For the past two hundred years mankind has been busy domesticating a philosophical approach to the universe worked out in Greece some 2500 years ago. This approach is called the scientific method. The development and implementation of this method has given us industrialization, engineering and technology, a breathtaking rise in the standard of living of many (but nowhere near all) people, methods for maintaining extremely high population levels, and much, much more. Our lives would be radically different without science.
　　So would our literature. I intend to view detective stories, science fiction, and fantasy as reactions to the scientific revolution of the past two hundred years. The first key name here is Edgar Allan Poe. Like Dickens and Dostoevski, Poe was a magazine writer. He invented the detective story; he wrote enough science fiction to fill a decent-sized volume; and his horror stories are well-known to us all. Poe's detective, C. Auguste Dupin, appeared in three stories: "The Murders in the Rue Morgue" (1841), "The Mystery of Marie Roget" (1842-3), and "The Purloined Letter" (1844). In their Introduction to their superb anthology, The Great American Detective, William Kittredge and Steven M. Krauzer point out that Dupin "is eccentric in the extreme; were he not a brilliant practitioner of the art of ratiocination, he would likely be put away as a lunatic." And they continue, "Poe is correctly credited with inventing nearly all the conventions of the detective story, of which two stand out as most important. The first [is] Dupin's incredible powers of reasoning and intellect. . . . [The second is that] he is the only character capable of success." None of the other characters can use those mental features Poe calls the "analytical"; that is, Poe's detective differs from other men, not only in his eccentricities of behavior, but also in his ability to think rationally and scientifically. And this, it seems to me, is the value---perhaps even the raison d'etre--of the detective

story from Poe on: it presents in popular form the delights and achievements made possible by rational, orderly thinking. The detective story is one way the scientific method is spread and popularized. Even today, large numbers of people who earn their livings with various applications of rational thought--doctors, teachers, engineers---enjoy an evening in the company of Dupin and Holmes, Hercule Poirot and Nero Wolfe. They understand one another because they think alike.

Science fiction too disseminates an understanding of and an appreciation for rational thinking. In Larry Niven's "Neutron Star," for example, Beowulf Schaeffer is alone in an experimental spaceship plunging along a preplanned orbit deeper and deeper into the gravity well of a neutron star. A similar experiment has already killed two researchers on a previous expedition, and Beowulf knows he will die too---unless he can figure out what the mysterious force which threatens him is and how to neutralize it. He goes over one piece of data after another, constructs explanation after explanation. Then he performs an experiment. He goes to the center of gravity of the ship and releases two objects, one in front of him, one behind. Both fall away from him, one in each direction. Now he knows what the deadly force is and what to do about it. Do we? The fun of solving an abstract intellectual puzzle in this story is just as great as in any detective story. The deadly force is later described as "tidal." The front of the ship is pointed directly at the neutron star, and the difference in tidal effects from the front to the rear, tremendously intensified by the neutron star's intense gravity, threatens to pull the ship in half. Anyone either in the front or the back would be crushed against the walls, as the first two scientists had been. Beowulf Schaeffer fights to stay in the balance point between the two tidal forces, succeeds, and lives. Know the scientific method, and the scientific method shall save your life. Like Dupin or Holmes, Beowulf thinks rationally to solve a problem; and in doing so, he shows the readers how it's done and so disseminates the scientific, rational, "analytical" way of thinking.

Admittedly most science fiction doesn't work this way. In most science fiction the characters must learn to deal, not with rational thinking itself, but with the results of rational thinking applied to the physical environment--that is, with the products of engineering and technology. Thus we have the paraphernalia of science fiction seen on dustjackets and covers: rocketships, rayguns, robots, time machines, domed cities and so forth. How would life be different if science-- the application of rational thought to the environment-- eventually made available to us a matter transmitter or a time viewer, an operation to make us super-intelligent or an electronic implant that put us in instantaneous contact with computer banks stocked with whatever data we wanted? Rational thought itself is not the raison d'etre of these stories, but dealing with the results of rational thought is. My argument here is really that old chestnut ("science fiction prepares its readers for change") in a slightly different form. What caused the change that we need scientific fiction to prepare us for? Science, the scientific method, engineering and technology, that's what.

The method by which the science fiction writer achieves the willing suspension of disbelief, the method by which he makes his oddities plausible and realistic, was developed by H. G. Wells, most clearly perhaps in the first chapter of The Time Machine. You coat what is a present impossibility, such as a matter transmitter, in the milk chocolate of scientific-sounding gobbledygook so that the reader can swallow it. (As Somerset Maugham, I think it was, used to say, "Plausibility is what you can get your readers to swallow.") Wells made the scientifically implausible idea of time travel seem plausible, and other writers in the tradition have followed him and thereby made time travel a staple of science fiction rather than of fantasy. The same has happened with faster-than-light drives, other dimensions and parallel/alternate worlds, and secret hidden powers of the human mind, such as telepathy, telekinesis, precognition. None of these things are in the established, respectable canon of modern scientific belief; but all of them are accepted as "scientific" within science fiction because H. G. Wells invented a technique for making them scientific-sounding and because in science fiction tradition so many writers now have followed Wells's example.

I am now treading the borderline between science fiction and fantasy. Personally, I distinguish between the two this way: science fiction makes use of scientifically plausible settings, and fantasy makes use of scientifically implausible settings. That is, science fiction assumes that the modern scientific worldview is correct and works within it. Fantasy ignores the modern scientific worldview and builds its own self-consistent worlds. For the science fiction writer, the laws of nature as presently understood and formulated are a given to be taken into account in the creation of worlds and stories; for the fantasy writer, they are not. The science fiction writer has a universe ready at hand to work in; the fantasy writer must always start from scratch.

Fantasy seems to be becoming more and more popular these days. Let me suggest two reasons. First, fantasy can be viewed as a reaction against the modern scientific worldview. On the one hand, this worldview is a difficult and complex one, hard to learn and become comfortable in. Many people still insist they cannot learn science and math. They don't want to be members of the modern world, except by accident of birth, because it's too hard. So fantasy, for some, is an escape from the rigors of modern science. More importantly, I think, on the other hand, what science studies, codifies, understands is merely the lowest common denominator of human experience. Gray's Anatomy describes the disposition of your intestines, the workings of your heart and liver and lungs, whether or not your name is Gray. No matter who you are, if you have a certain mass and fall a certain distance (from a windowledge or a stepladder, say), you will strike the ground with the same momentum. Swift once personified the detached impersonality of the scientist this way: "I saw a woman flayed alive the other day, and you would scarcely believe how it altered her appearance for the worse." Indeed; but how did she feel? And how ought we to feel towards her? Fantasy, I suggest, is increasingly attractive these days as an alternative to the difficulty and/or the inhumanity of the modern scientific worldview.

But a second reason also exists. Fantasy exploits the irrational side of modern science. In his article on Heisenberg in his Biographical Encyclopedia of Science and Technology, Isaac Asimov rather casually remarks, "[Heisenberg's uncertainty principle, first stated in 1927] had the effect of weakening the law of cause and effect, which . . . had been an unquestioned and unstudied anchor of science since the days of Thales and the Ionian philosophers. Heisenberg's uncertainty principle destroyed the purely deterministic philosophy of the universe." "Even Einstein," Asimov writes further down, "found himself uncomfortable with this new way of looking at the universe." In his essay "In the Beginning . . ." (published as a chapter in A Step Farther Out), Jerry Pournelle writes of his having heard Stephen Hawking, one of the leading theoretical physicists of our time, point out that "what comes out [of a singularity] is completely random, absolutely uncorrelated. This [is a] fundamental breakdown in prediction. Hawking is saying not only that we can't predict now, but that in principle we can never predict, no matter how much we know or how smart we get or how large a computer we build." Farther on, Pournelle writes, "We've just heard one of the top people in theoretical physics tell us that we don't know anything and can't know anything; that causality is a local phenomenon of purely temporary nature." (Isn't that last a lovely phrase: "causality is a local phenomenon of purely temporary nature.") And he concludes, "Our rational universe is crumbling. Western civilization assumes reason; that some things are impossible, that's all; that the universe is at least in principle discoverable by the human reason, is knowable . . . That, says one of the men we believe best understands this universe, is not true." The modern scientific worldview contains in it a perfect rationale for fantasy.

To sum up my argument to this point, then, the detective story became popular after Poe invented it in 1841 because it provides entertaining teachers to the general public and sympathetic companions to those who already know and use rational thought in their daily lives. Science fiction also provides illustrative examples of the scientific method in action, but primarily it shows people dealing with the possible products of scientific and technological progress. Fantasy is a reaction against the scientific worldview by people who find that view too difficult and/or too inhumane, while fantasy also exploits the irrational side of our Western European rational view of the universe.

This brings us to horror stories and to Stephen King. Horror stories are a form of fantasy. Modern scientific thought, verbalized by people like Stephen Hawking, tells us that a singularity can radiate anything: an exact duplicate of Harlan Ellison, Cthulhu, a new value for pi. We must be prepared for anything. This is exactly what horror stores tell us. In his Foreword to Night Shift, Stephen King speaks of the horror writer "talking about the way the good fabric of things sometimes has a way of unraveling with shocking suddenness." The rational side of science assures us that we understand where we are, that we're secure, in control; that if something seems strange and puzzling, a little more research and we'll have it safely categorized and cause-and-effected. The universe makes sense. And if something about it doesn't make sense, the problem's not with the universe, but with our understanding, with the state of our knowledge. But Stephen Hawking says that causality is a local phenomenon of purely temporary nature and our rational view of the universe is crumbling. And Stephen King says that the good fabric of things sometimes has a way of unraveling with shocking suddenness. The theoretical physicist and the pop lit writer are both telling us the same thing. Permit me to quote a bit from the Foreword to King's Night Shift.

> The horror writer always brings bad news: you're going to die he says; he's telling you to never mind Oral Roberts and his 'something good is going to happen to you,' because something bad is going to happen to you, and it may be cancer and it may be a stroke and it may be a car accident, but it's going to happen. And he takes your hand and he enfolds it in his own, and he takes you into the room and he puts your hands on the shape under the sheet . . . and tells you to touch it here . . . here . . . and here. . . . It is the shape of a body under [that] sheet. All our fears add up to one great fear, all our fears are part of that great fear. . . . We're afraid of the body under the sheet. It's our body. And the great appeal of horror fiction through the ages is that it serves as a rehearsal for our own deaths.

So Stephen King is surely a fantasist, the kind who makes us face, in a variety of disguises, but still unmistakably and unavoidably, what each of us sees as the ultimate irrationality of the universe: our own personal deaths.

That leaves me still to talk about Stephen King the science fiction writer, and my time is gone. Permit me a few quick points. One: some of King's stuff is clearly and indisputably science fiction. The short story, "I Am the Doorway," for example, is about an astronaut returned from orbiting Venus and the curious disease he brings back with him. And The Stand: a mutated virus escapes the lab and kills 99.9 percent of the people on earth, and the survivors must band together to survive, a staple in science fiction at least since Mary Shalley's The Last Man.

A second point: when I started reading through King's books this summer (and I read all ten of them, including The Gunslinger, the Creepshow comic book, and Different Seasons) I began with Carrie. I didn't understand then (and I don't understand now) how anyone can read Carrie as anything other than science fiction. Carrie is not possessed; she is simply a young girl afflicted with secret hidden powers of the human mind, secret hidden powers that she is too young and immature and confused to control. Her secret hidden power is telekinesis, a wild talent we have all read about many times over the years. Actually, Carrie is a science fiction novel of the type discussed earlier, the type in which scientifically implausible things like faster-than-light drives and parallel worlds and time travel have been accepted into the science fiction canon because of the work of a whole tradition of writers since H. G. Wells.

A third point: King clearly likes children afflicted with secret hidden powers of the human mind. Beside Carrie, we have Danny Torrance in *The Shining*, Leo Rockway in *The Stand*, and of course the pyrokinetic Charlie McGee in *Firestarter*. Science fiction characters all, and King has read his science fiction and knows these characters. *Firestarter* contains this paragraph:

> . . . and still there was time to think about that story, the one he had read as a kid, "It's a Good Life!," by some guy named Jerome Bixby, and that had been about a little kid [named Little Anthony] who had enslaved his parents with psychic terror, a nightmare of a thousand possible deaths, and you never knew . . . you never knew when the little kid was going to get mad . . .

"It's a Good Life!" is in the *Science Fiction Hall of Fame*, Vol. I. It's one of the acknowledged classics in the field. And if it's science fiction, then so is *Carrie* and *Firestarter* and elements in *The Shining* and of course *The Stand* (for other reasons too). So it seems to me that we shouldn't forget that Stephen King, whatever else he may be, is also a science fiction writer.

One final "it seems to me" before I quit. Science fiction writers are constantly talking about "breaking out of category" to the big audience and therefore the big money. *Stranger in a Strange Land* and *Dune* were two of the first books to show that scientific novels could do this. One of the more fascinating things about what King has done is that he has found a new way to break out of category. He located and exploited an area where science fiction and occult/psychic/horror novels might be said to overlap. I really wonder how *Carrie* escaped being published as another 2500-copy "Doubleday SF line" novel. Was it King himself, or his agent, or the publisher who began packaging his science fiction novels as something else so that they sell millions of copies to people who never read science fiction? Pulling off this marketing coup may just be the most fantastic thing Stephen King has yet done.

University of Dayton

Richard Law

Science Fiction Women: Victims, Rebels, Heroes

In the Poetics, Aristotle observes that poetry, or literature, is philosophical inasmuch as it reliably imitates or represents universals, that is, general concepts about what people say and do, according to probability. From this Aristotelian standpoint I shall comment on several pieces of science fiction by women, focusing for the sake of unity on just one question among the many raised in the works. It is the question of woman as maker (in the productive role) and woman as mother (in the reproductive role). Each role is complex and might be assumed simultaneously or alternately by one person or another. But for clear discussion, although risking oversimplification, the two roles will be regarded as separate.
In De Generatione Animalium, II.i, Aristotle ponders the respective places of women and men in reproduction:

> It is better that the superior principle should be separated from the inferior. Therefore, wherever it is possible and so far as it is possible, the male is separated from the female. For the first principle of movement, or efficient cause, whereby that which comes into being is male, is better and more divine than the material whereby it is female. The male, however, comes together and mingles with the female for the work of generation, because this is common to both.[1]

Evidently, Aristotle is not infallible. Yet this erroneous and invidious proposition held sway longer than two millenia and is not at all laid to rest even now. In Joanna Russ' fiction the base assumption is continually attacked, nowhere more vehemently than in the novel/anti-novel, The Female Man (1975). Just one of many combative passages in the book is this, part of a nightmare of a conventionally conditioned "old-fashioned girl":

> . . . if that isn't guilt, what is?. . . . I knew it was
> not wrong to be a girl because Mommy said so; cunts were
> all right if they were neutralized, one by one, by being
> hooked on to a man, but this orthodox arrangement only
> partly redeems them and every biological possessor of one
> knows in her bones that radical inferiority which is only
> another name for Original Sin.
>   Pregnancy, for example . . . , it's a disaster, but
> we're too enlightened to blame the woman for her perfect-
> ly natural behavior, aren't we? Only keep it secret and
> keep it going--and I'll give you three guesses as to which
> partner the pregnancy is in.[2]

The old-fashioned girl's guilt-ridden nightmare testifies to the age-old, grueling struggle for redress and respect. In Russ' Nebula Award-winning story, "When It Changed" (1972), women who survive a plague which kills the entire male population on the planet Whileaway adapt capably and learn to merge ova for propagation. During 600 years, the women have developed a self-reliant, versatile, progressive society. Then an expedition of men from Earth arrives; the leader declares that men are obviously needed to complete the species. Janet, the narrator, expresses her melancholy meditation that if both sexes reunite, it will, to judge by past history, mean women will again be subjugated.[3]

With or without joining battle, other women writers of science fiction besides Joanna Russ reflect on the actual handicaps of women, as well as on the subordinate status which is perceived or is imposed on them because (for one reason) they bear children. Pamela Zoline's "The Heat Death of the Universe," often reprinted since first publication in 1967, is about a day in the life of a mother whose inexorable responsibilities and frustrations have driven her to the nervous breakdown which the story charts.[4] The fifty-four paragraphs are numbered so as to give the effect of a relentless countdown to nervous breakdown. In paragraph 9, Sarah Boyle is identified as a vivacious, intelligent, cultured woman proud of her growing family. In paragraph 14, she writes this message in lipstick on the wall by the washing machine: "Many young wives feel trapped. It is a contemporary sociological phenomenon which may be explained in part by a gap between changing living patterns and the accommodation of social services to these patterns." Poignant irony. The wives "feel trapped"? They are trapped, whether or not they behave like Sarah Boyle. She loses count of how many children she has, she cried uncontrollably and shatters glasses and dishes, and in an alarmingly symbolic act in paragraph 54, she takes eggs out of the refrigerator and throws them one by one onto the kitchen floor.

Judith Merril's "That Only a Mother" was first published in Campbell's Astounding Science Fiction in 1948; it appears in many anthologies, including The Science Fiction Hall of Fame, Vol. I. Its anti-atomic war theme is prominent, but the title, "That Only a Mother," announces its other major concern. This story also depicts a mother becoming unhinged. By the end of the story, Mrs. Hank Marvell's husband finally comes home on military leave expecting to find the precocious baby his wife had been celebrating in letters to him. Seeing for the first time their abnormal ten-month old infant, Hank reacts to it and to his psychoneurotic wife:

> Maggie, why didn't you tell me? . . . She didn't know.
> His hands, beyond control, ran up and down the soft-
> skinned baby body, the sinuous, limbless body. Oh God,
> dear God--his head shook and his muscles contracted in
> a bitter spasm of hysteria. His fingers tightened on
> his child--Oh God, she didn't know . . .[5]

Judith Merrill's story and Pamela Zoline's amplify the predicament of the confined mother, starved for adult company and desperate for the personal interest and shared caring of husband/father. Maggie's husband, Lt. Hank Marvell, is away most of the time, and Sarah Boyle's husband never appears in the story. The tacit abandonment of Sarah and Maggie and their distress are true-to-life. One infers from both stories corroboration of Joanna Russ' protest against the segregation and subordination of present-day Penelopes. The inequitable conditions reflected in these and other domestic science fiction pieces can be condensed into two columns, allowing for some exceptions and adjustments. Column one has these terms: free, independent, voluntary, creative or productive, intellectual, and public. Opposite terms belong in the second column: unfree, dependent, obligatory, procreative or reproductive, natural, and private. The polarity I have itemized underscores the age-old denial of opportunities for women in public and cultural sectors. In "The Heat Death of the Universe," Sarah Boyle contemplates the artistic explosion that would result from the abolition of motherhood: "the race would extinguish itself in a fair sweet flowering, the last generations' massive achievement in the arts and pursuits of high civilization." This is an oversimplified and exaggerated dream, of course, but not without a measure of validity.

Besides imposing demeaning duties and status on women, historically, bearing young has also reinforced the pejorative association of women with animality. In The Word for World Is Forest (1972), Ursula LeGuin deplores the machismo drive to dominate women, and aliens, and nature. Captain Don Davidson, the macho military frontiersman, makes this appraisal of the women transported twenty-seven lightyears from Earth: "the new shipload of women had arrived. . . . the second batch of breeding females for the New Tahiti Colony, all sound and clean, 212 head of prime human stock. Or prime enough, anyhow."[6] Most of the men in the colony amiably label the women "Collie Girls."

The woman-mother-animal cognation has been exposed frequently by Alice Sheldon (James Tiptree, Jr.), and with most lethal irony in her 1973 story, "The Women Men Don't See." A plane carrying two men and two women crashlands in a swamp in Yucatan. Three extraterrestrials also arrive there, and Ruth Parsons and her daughter depart with them, foreseeing that the aliens' world will be more hospitable for them than Earth is. The text frequently correlates the women and animals. Together in a hammock, they are "cozy in their chilly ibis roost."[7] Mrs. Parsons is "Mother Hen protecting only chick from male predators." Mrs. Parsons tells Don Fenton that even the new rights of women obtain only with the sufferance of men, who are "more aggressive and powerful and run the world." Even resourceful women like her merely survive "in the chinks of [man's] world-machine." "Think of us as opossums," she says, "Did you know there are opossums living all over? Even in New York City." After mother and daughter are gone, Don obtusely wonders why: "She'd meant every word. Insane. How could a woman choose to live among unknown monsters, to say good-bye to her home, her world?" He remembers watching them depart in the darkness and thinks, "Two of our opossums are missing."

Several decades ago, the great psychologist-philosopher, William James, divided philosophers into two general dispositions: the tough-minded and the tender-minded. Alice Sheldon's tough-minded science fiction reflects a philosophical bent that is empiricist, antiromantic, unspiritual, skeptical, and pessimistic. Russ' fiction is uncompromising but seems less toughminded because of its intimate confessional nature, its distress, its urgent appeal and heartbreak. By comparison, Sheldon's stories seem generated by calm, concentrated rhetorical power. Conversely, the tender-minded philosopher will be rationalistic, and given to theory and principles more than hard facts; romantic or idealistic; positive; and comparatively optimistic. The tender-minded disposition is reflected in the fiction of Kate Wilhelm.

"April Fools' Day Forever" is a Jungian story, almost by definition tender-minded. Wilhelm acknowledged writing it in order to concretize "the paranoia of pregnancy."[8] Julia Sayre is a promising sculptor and a mother-to-be, hence a creator and procreator, producing art and reproducing life. She also is nearly totally dependent on men for her practical well-being: her husband (Martie), his male boss, her landlord, the mailman, her several doctors, an influential art critic, etc. The story deals with Julia's escape from a conspiracy that she knows about intuitively. Some doctors and experts in genetics are deciding which newborn babies can benefit from an immortality serum and which ones, along with their mothers, should be terminated. But the conspiracy is dispelled and the story ends happily. Julia has completed a Jungian sculpture, organic and mystical; and she and her husband rejoice in it and in the newborn baby boy.

Like many other pieces by Kate Wilhelm, "April Fools' Day Forever" is not iconoclastic. It takes a flawed male-dominated social system for granted but implicitly proposes a private, personal, interdependent union of woman and man as the ideal human relationship and as a metaphysical symbol of benevolent harmony. Woman, man, and child enjoy reciprocal human values; their mutual welfare with dignity is not a panacea in an imperfect world but is the matrix of higher values: shared love and caring. In Wilhelm's idealistic sphere, woman can develop artistic potential and also happily satisfy maternal desires.

In her award-winning novel, <u>Where Late the Sweet Birds Sang</u> (1976), Wilhelm idealizes the exclusive love relationship between a woman and man as the indispensable and estimable way of preserving the species (contrary to other theories of pairing or alternative methods of reproduction that science fiction entertains). In the first of the three sections of the novel, David and Celia are innocent, fated lovers in the Romeo and Juliet tradition. Their love is a fragile human value facing extinction along with the race: "We're finished, aren't we, David? You, I, all of us?" the dying young woman asks soon after she and David have united sexually.[9] In the sentimental epilogue of the novel, the reordaining of the human race is signaled by the joyous homecoming of Mark to Linda. "She was nineteen, large with child, his child." Motherhood is exalted in the poignant second section of Where Late the Sweet Birds Sang, in the person of Mark's mother, Molly. Both she and her love partner, Ben, are condemned because they are exhibiting human individualism with bonds of conjugal love in a society of clones. Molly is an artist who also makes an heroic effort to protect her son, Mark, just as Julia Sayre in "April Fools' Day Forever" defies the system that would threaten her unborn son.

Molly's clandestine painting (and her son's sculpting) symbolize precious creativity; her nurturing is equally esteemed, and her reunion (in death) with Ben is represented as transcendental absorption in Nature: "together they floated down, down into the cool, sweet water." Molly (and to a lesser degree the other women with normal sensibilities) defers to her mate without losing dignity; and Ben, and David and Mark, reflect a sense of responsibility, respect, and gratitude that is exemplary. In this post-Doomsday, new-Edenic novel, the focus is not on man and woman in conventional society, but on their personal interrelationship under abnormal conditions after nuclear holocaust. From the standpoint of poetic imagination and life science, in Ms. Wilhelm's depiction of humans returned to a state of Nature, Molly personifies the archetype that Jung's protege, Erich Neumann, brilliantly analyzed. For example, Neumann writes this:

> Thus the Feminine, the giver of nourishment, becomes everywhere a revered principle of nature, on which man is dependent in pleasure and pain. It is from this eternal experience of man, who is as helpless in his dependence on nature as the infant in his dependence on his mother, that the mother-child figure is inspired forever anew.[10]

Anthropology, psychology, and cultural history notwithstanding, the myth of "the Great Mother" is not complementary, not even palatable, to Joanna Russ' victims and rebels. A passage late in The Female Man alludes to aspects of the archetype (which has been glorified for two generations of undergraduates). The narrator, Joanna, who is a strikingly transparent persona, recalls learning in college that "Woman is the gateway to another world; Woman is the earth-mother; Woman is the life-force. . . . Joanna reduces this standard litany to absurdity by trying the grand terms on herself:

> I am the gateway to another world, (said I, looking in the mirror) I am the earth-mother; I am the eternal siren; I am purity, (Jeez, new pimples) I am carnality; I have intuition; I am the life-force; I am selfless love. (Somehow it sounds different in the first person, doesn't it?)
>
> Honey (said the mirror, scandalized) Are you out of your fuckin' mind?[11]

Russ writes in the current idiom, including vulgar expressions and invective; she also writes forcefully, clearly, and strongly subjectively. Consequently, many readers have overemphasized the angry tone and sense of personal disturbance in her work.[12] As a matter of fact, the arsenal of tropes so effectively used by Russ is evidence of burning idealism, an absolute conviction that age-old habits of mind and behavior must be changed radically if women are ever to enjoy real freedom and equality--not promises and Mother's Day sanctimony.[13]

Not so polemical as The Female Man, although just as fervent, is We Who Are About To (1975), a vivid, dramatic monologue by a distressed woman who scorns being perceived as a "walking womb."[14] Elaine is with a small group of men and women stranded on an isolated planet. She alienates herself by insisting that they resign themselves to imminent doom, and she abandons the party once the men decide that for survival and colonization they must impregnate the women, including Elaine--by raping her, if she will not comply. After a few days, everyone but the fugitive is dead, five of them killed by Elaine, including Professor Ude, proponent of Woman's reproductive servitude, and Alan-Bobby, primitive virility personified.

Elaine's acts of violence for self-defense are significant philosophically. The sexist tyranny she destroyed symbolizes a socio-economic system which thrives on fierce competition and equates raw power and aggression with superiority. She defied and defeated the "Upper Paleolithic" men whose women would subserve their crazy dream of siring a new patriarchy with the old evils implicitly justified on the assumption that might makes right. Subsequently, Elaine kills herself rather than wait for slow, ghastly death. But before applying the contact poison, she records a moving examination of conscience that reviews the conditions to which she could never be reconciled: class privilege, exploitation and oppression of women, all manifestations of macho mentality, and every denial of social and political equality. Elaine's suicide, understandable under the circumstances, also verifies the protest preserved in printed form on her pocket "vocorder." It is an expression of despair by a woman who rejected life under a dispensation to which she knew women should not acquiese. Her isolation and self-destruction signify, too, the loneliness and futility of existence on Earth, which Elaine ironically calls "Kind old home. The sweetheart. The darling place. Think of Death Valley . . . in August."[14]

Joan D. Vinge is another science fiction writer attuned to Existentialism, but her isolated or beleaguered characters survive what William Barrett calls the modern "encounter with Nothingness."[15] A representative character is Emmylou Stewart in the homiletic story, "View from a Height." Lacking natural immunities essential for life on Earth, Emmylou volunteered for permanent duty as an explorer isolated in an observatory in space. Being "trapped in the arc of blackness . . . meaningless, so insignificant," she falls into depression but recovers and expresses valiant acquiescence: "We're all on a one-way trip into infinity. If we're lucky we're given some life's work we care about, or some person. Or both, if we're very lucky."[16]

Optimistic fatalism is the prevailing attitude in the work of Vinge. Her strength is the romance, a genre older than the novel--"a fact which has developed," in Northrop Frye's words, "the historical illusion that it is something to be outgrown, a juvenile and undeveloped form."[17] Without denying the existence of evil or the data of suffering, this tender-minded author highlights innocence and beauty, which belong to human experience as surely as do their opposites. She recalls treasured impressions--allusions to fairy tales and childhood memories are frequent--and commends the endearing or admirable traits in men, women, and children. Underlying her sentimental science fiction fables is a steadfast belief in the power of the human spirit to endure pain, promote decency, and preserve love.

Whether it is a reflective piece, a long exotic fantasy like The Snow Queen, or a juvenile space adventure, nearly every work by Joan Vinge is a love story, sentimental and idealized, but not to be confused with silly television and film servings. Most of her characters who love are not glamorous or handsome; some are permanently disabled, some are deformed, some are freaks. They have been losers and might never be much better than survivors; and their love, no matter how poetic, will not dissolve the hard conditions of existence. Love is not a panacea, not perpetual ecstasy, and not a magic charm in Vinge's fiction. It is emotional interdependence, mutual commitment, caring and sacrifice shared. The Outcasts of Heaven Belt (1978) is a light space-adventure entertainment.[18] It also is designed to address its epigraph from Ecclesiastes: "Two are better than one, because they have a good reward for their labours. For if they fall, the one will lift up his fellow: but woe to him that is alone when he falleth; for he hath not another to help him up." The ideal of unity in adversity is sensitively exhibited by two fugitives, Shadow Jack, a certified defective, and Bird Alyn, rejected as an ugly, ungainly cripple. Mutual empathy upholds them: "She had comforted him, out of compassion and her own need; his need had bound him to her, and made them friends." They and other couples in Joan Vinge's works illustrate the concept that "the unifying element, the common bond of need that join[s] every human being, could be used as a force against disintegration and decay."

Through much of the dialogue in The Outcasts of Heaven Belt, the concept of the "multiple-marriage family unit" is explained. In the discussion, it is acknowledged that the keystone of this innovative form is traditional conjugality. It is assumed that every woman and man in the multiple marriage will try to maintain a balanced distribution of rewards and sacrifices, domestic responsibilities and public duties. With this thesis, the novel is like a wish fulfillment dream. After the threat to Ranger is over and the starship is heading home, Bird Alyn and Shadow Jack are married by the captain in a small old-fashioned ceremony with the exchange of wedding rings. Betha Torgussen, the captain, is an outstanding engineer; she also is a dedicated wife and mother.

Notwithstanding her pipe-smoking and take-charge ability, Betha is self-conscious about her role as commander. Her basic emotional responses are those of the distaff (not a disadvantage in her society). After her beloved first husband, Eric, is killed in a space skirmish, Betha finds succor in the sheltering arms of her uncle, Clewell. He is the second of her husbands and is nearly twice Betha's age; she affectionately calls him "Pappy." She and Eric had shared a monogamous marriage for eight years, and they had had twins, before uniting with Clewell's family. Betha constantly laments the loss of Eric and regrets being away from the children at home. Gradually she falls in love with Wadie Abdiamal, an interplanetary negotiator, who seems like another Eric; "But he's not Eric. He's not one of us, he's one of them. How can I feel this way?" During the sentimental conclusion of the adventure, Clewell foresees her marriage to Wadie, "a good man, . . . the right man. Like another good man who had loved his wife and been his friend."

The Outcasts of Heaven Belt is a marriage and family fairy tale. It is true that for sentimental style of expression, the poetic allusions, soothing reflections, the regard for innocence and domesticity, for children and gentle animals, nearly all of Vinge's science fiction has a fairy tale ambience. But the need for faith and hope and the benefits of human interdependence reflected in her works are true-to-life. Joan Vinge speaks to the imagination in a transitional age that psychotherapist Rollo May diagnoses as suffering "bankruptcy of inner values." For lack of love and will, the contemporary world is schizoid. Those attributes are necessary for people who yearn to exercise "the conjunctive emotions and processes." The source of love and will is care, concern, compassion:

> Care is a state composed of the recognition of another, a fellow human being like one's self; of identification of one's self with the pain or joy of the other; of guilt, pity, and the awareness that we all stand on the base of a common humanity. . . . Care is given power by nature's sense of pain. . . and care must become a conscious psychological fact.[19]

Vinge and Kate Wilhelm both idealize the conjugal relationship in which a woman and man, with or without children, are united in care. But care is an attribute that seems so rare historically and today that its efficacy is dubious to Joanna Russ and Alice Sheldon. They depict the consequent alienation and aggression in a society that continues to assume that woman's place is subordinate to man's. The tough-minded science fiction writers expose the thoughtless assumptions and philosophical rationalizations supporting the age-old sexist order. The tender-minded imagine models of love in a better order--at least a retreat--wherein harmony between the sexes is cultivated.

Kutztown State College

Notes

[1] Aristotle, *De Generatione Animalium*, II.i, in *The Works of Aristotle*, V, ed. J. A. Smith and W. D. Ross (London: Oxford U. Press, 1912; 1958), 732^a.

[2] Joanna Russ, *The Female Man* (New York: Bantam Books, 1975; 1978).

[3] Russ, "When It Changed," in *The Road to Science Fiction #3*, ed. James Gunn (New York: New American Library, 1979).

[4] Pamela Zoline, "The Heat Death of the Universe," in *The Mirror of Infinity*, ed. Robert Silverberg (New York: Harper and Row, 1970).

[5] Judith Merril, "That Only a Mother," in *Women of Wonder*, ed. Pamela Sargent (New York: Random House Vintage Books, 1975).

[6] Ursula K. LeGuin, *The Word for World is Forest* (New York: Berkley Publishing Corp., 1972; 1976).

[7] James Tiptree, Jr., "The Women Men Don't See," in *Warm Worlds and Otherwise* (New York: Ballantine Books, 1975).

[8] Kate Wilhelm, "April Fools' Day Forever," in *The Infinity Box* (New York: Pocket Books, 1977), xi.

[9] Wilhelm, *Where Late the Sweet Birds Sang* (New York: Pocket Books, 1976).

[10] Erich Neumann, *The Great Mother: An Analysis of the Archetype*, 2nd ed. (Princeton, New Jersey: The Princeton University Press, 1963), p. 131.

[11] *The Female Man*.

[12] See Michael Goodwin's review. Goodwin acknowledges that the book is important although he "hated it for months"; it is a "bitter fantasy of reversed sexual oppression" "One Giant Step for Science Fiction," *Mother Jones*, I, no. 6 (August, 1976), 62. Bruce Kawin's judgment is not antagonistic: "It is clear that Russ considers anger a healing force not just for her character-selves but for herself as an artist." See *The Mind of the Novel: Reflexive Fiction and the Ineffable* (Princeton, 1982), p. 317.

[13] A model critical preparation for *The Female Man* would be the essay of Jonathan Swift which Herbert Davis wrote at mid century. Swift uses "a directness, and force, and plainness to make sure that even the sleepiest . . . might know exactly what instruction" is coming. See "The Conciseness of Swift," in *Jonathan Swift: Essays on His Satire and Other Studies)* New York: Oxford University Press, 1964), pp. 216-233.

[14] Joanna Russ, *We Who Are About To . . .* (New York: Dell

Publishing Co., 1977). The discussion here follows an exchange of impressions with Professor Judith Spector, who has written about gender-related conflict ("Dr. Jekyll and Mrs. Hyde") in Joanna Russ' novels.

[15] William Barrett, *Irrational Man: A Study in Existential Philosophy* (Garden City, New York: Doubleday and Co., 1962), p. 23.

[16] Joan D. Vinge, "View from a Height," in *"Eyes of Amber" and Other Stories* (New York: New American Library, 1979). Part of the discussion here of Ms. Vinge's work was previously presented in a session, "Stellar Women in Science Fiction," at the 1981 NCTE Convention in Boston.

[17] Northrop Frye, *Anatomy of Criticism* (Atheneum, New York: Atheneum Paperbacks, 1965), p. 306.

[18] Vinge, *The Outcasts of Heaven Belt* (New York: The New American Library, 1978).

[19] Rollo May, *Love and Will* (New York: W. W. Norton, 1979), pp. 10, 14, and 289.

Jim Villani

           The Woman Science Fiction Writer
            and the Non-Heroic Male Protagonist

    The cult of heroism is as old as literature. The figure
of the hero is resurrected and adored by each generation of
new writers. We identify literature by its heroes; they
excite us and motivate us. Even the subjective and stream-
of-consciousness literatures of the twentieth century have
failed to stamp out the influence of the hero. The cult of
the hero remains strong in mainstream literature and especially in genre literature, such as in science fiction, which has
been heavily influenced by pulp and comic book super heroes,
and which continues to produce daring, resourceful gallants
such as Captain Kirk of <u>Star Trek</u> or Luke Skywalker of <u>Star
Wars</u>. Science fiction fandom anticipates and even demands
heroes.
    Although the hero has a long and popular history, there
are many examples of the non-heroic type, or anti-hero,
existing side-by-side with the great heroes of literature.
In the genre of science fiction, where the protagonist is
usually male and almost always an heroic type, it is woman
writers who have exercised the greatest flexibility in the
treatment of the male protagonist. Women writers have
created many non-heroic male protagonists; in so doing they
present a distinctly feminist viewpoint and offer a more
objective view of male behavior than that promulgated by
male writers. In so doing, women science fiction writers
have gently but thoroughly politicized the genre with the
modern spirit of feminism.
    The prototype of the science fiction hero is the swagger-
ing, romantic valiant of adventure and frontier literature.
Borrowing directly from this tradition, C. L. Moore embraced
the pattern for the contemporary science fiction hero when
she created, in 1933, the enigmatic and mysterious space
outlaw, Northwest Smith:

    Smith, lounging negligently against the wall, arms

folded and gun-hand draped over his left-forearm, looking incapable of swift motion, but at the leader's first forward step the pistol swept in a practiced half-circle and the dazzle of blue-white heat leaping from its muzzle seared an arc in the slag pavement at his feet. It was an old gesture, and not a man in the crowd but understood it . . .

"Are you crossing that line?" queried Smith in an ominously gentle voice.[1]

But C. L. Moore is a woman, and her exciting, stalwart protagonist, for all his attractive bravado, is a caricature of the epic hero. Women science fiction writers often remain curiously aloof from the hypnotic sway of the male hero. They have created alternatives to the epic hero, and in the process have generated some of the most remarkable psychological inquiries into the nature of male behavior. Women science fiction writers have successfully demythed the male hero by creating protagonists that don't behave like heroes. I shall examine this phenomenon more closely in four specific works by women science fiction writers spanning 160 years: Frankenstein, by Mary Wollstonecraft Shelley; "Shambleau," by C. L. Moore; Where Late The Sweet Birds Sang, by Kate Wilhelm; and The Dispossessed, by Ursula K. LeGuin.

These four works, although widely separated by time, style and plot, demonstrate a remarkable consistency in their attitudes towards the male hero. In fact, they successfully demyth the male hero by utilizing an identical anti-heroic mythical prototype as a blueprint for the male protagonist. The figure is that of Prometheus and its impact on these four works is not only pronounced, but also profound. Four different male protagonists are subjected to the primal Promethian error and are duly punished for their transgressions. The male hero emerges as an inherently flawed individual. In addition to the pattern of interference and punishment, the male protagonists in these works are carefully formed to contrast the prevailing traits of the epic hero in three important behavioral categories--intelligence, motivation and sexuality.

Nineteen-year-old Mary Wollstonecraft Godwin traveled to Switzerland in search of the romantic spirit. The young woman spent long evenings listening to the poets Shelley and Byron discuss the creative impulse, the origin and meaning of life, and the prevailing scientific advancements of the day. When she retired to her rooms, she worked diligently on her first novel, Frankenstein, or the Modern Prometheus. Typified as a gothic romance, it has been sequestered in a kind of critical graveyard, but the story itself, the creation of a pitiful monster who destroys its maker, has become a part of the popular imagination. By using the metaphor of the scientist and by embracing a prevalent scientific notion of her day, that of the quasi-electrical nature of life, Mary Shelley authored a penetrating psychological study of responsibility and failure through the character of Victor Frankenstein.

Mary Shelley adopted the figure of Prometheus from Byron and Shelley, who utilized the figure in their poetry as an emblem of the artist and the creative impulse. Mary applied the idea to the scientist and thereby greatly increased the moral ramification of the story. There are two principal versions of the myth.[2] In the most popular, Prometheus is a Titan who succors man by stealing fire from Zeus and delivering it to the mortals. The second version portrays Prometheus as a demigod who creates man from a bit of clay. Outraged, Zeus punishes Prometheus for his insolence, chaining him to a mountain where an eagle daily feeds on his liver. Each night the liver resuscitates as fast as the eagle could devour it by day. Shelley conceived Victor Frankenstein as a modern Prometheus, a scientist who discovers the secret of life (the providence of God) and blindly unleashes his discovery without due consideration of the consequences to himself or society. Once created, Victor spurns his creation and condemns himself: "Cursed be the day, abhorred devil, in which you first saw light! Cursed (although I curse myself) be the hands that formed you!"[3] Rejected and misplaced in society, the artificial man turns into a murderous fiend and eventually leads Frankenstein to his own death. Shelley's Victor Frankenstein is in every aspect a tragic hero. He is a man of promise and power who cannot control power; he pays a heavy price for his failure, losing family, best friend, wife and ultimately his own life. The Promethean cycle of interference and punishment is complete. The male protagonist is revealed as an anti-hero, misguided, vulnerable and guilty of an unpardonable sin.

The three twentieth-century works to be discussed each in their own way recreate the Promethean pattern. In "Shambleau," C. L. Moore makes a deliberate association between the shambleau and the mythical Medusa. But is not Northwest Smith himself a type of Prometheus? When Smith rescues the shambleau from a bloodthirsty mob in the Martian city of Taakdarrol, he inadvertently gives life to a monster every bit as hideous as that created by Victor Frankenstein. "We never let those things live" howled the ex-patrolman who led the mob, but Smith drives off the mob by declaring that the creature belongs to him. (Moore, p. 4). Just as Victor Frankenstein's monster obsessed the young scientist, Smith is obsessed and then possessed by an alien woman in a bizarre sexual parody. Frankenstein is punished for giving life to a monster; so too is Smith. In the end, the hero is demythed and Smith must be rescued by his partner, Yarol. Prometheus, too, it should be remembered, was eventually rescued and freed from his mountain prison by Heracles. Consequently, the rescued hero is another element of the Promethean cycle and of the concept of the anti-hero.

There are even stronger correspondences between Frankenstein and Kate Wilhelm's dystopian novel, Where Late The Sweet Birds Sang. David Sumner, also a young scientist, is the architect of a sophisticated cloning operation hidden away in the hills of Virginia. But the growing clone community shows little respect for the biological human beings. David becomes frustrated and dissatisfied with his creation: "It had been a mistake, David thought, watching the boys from the window. . . . 'They're inhuman, aren't they?' he said bitterly to Walt. . . . Clones! he said to himself vehemently. Clones! Not quite human. Clones."[4] He responds by trying to destroy the complicated computer system that monitors the sensitive laboratory breeding apparatus. He is foiled by the clones, exiled from the community and condemned to live alone in the desolate Virginia backwoods. Once again, the Promethean pattern of interference and punishment is applied to a brilliant young scientist who creates artificial life, only to become disheartened and to have his creation rebel against him. The Promethean anti-hero becomes the exiled hero, the man of prowess and sensibility and great dreams who sees all his ambition collapse around him in a fatal error and is driven away from his community.

One of the most innovative treatments of the Promethean cycle occurs in Ursula K. LeGuin's, The Dispossessed. In an interesting twist, LeGuin's Promethean type, Shevak, becomes an outcast before he produces his great creation, which is not a life-form, but a theory--the "General Temporal Theory" which will allow engineers to master "transilience," or faster than light travel. Like Victor and David, Shevak is a brilliant scientist. His dream is to unite the satellite worlds of Urras and Anarres by sharing his great scientific discovery. However, the citizens of Anarres, his home planet, reject him for his interest in Urras, and the political oligarchy that controls Urras attempts to arrogate the theory from Shevak so that they can control any emerging technology. The reader follows Shevak's adventures on two planets. On Anarres he is punished by detachment through the maneuvers of a strict communal orthodoxy, and on Urras his mobility is restricted by a greedy and conspiratorial political regime. But Shevak's real conflict is within himself. The modern Prometheus is an existential hero who faces an agonizing internal conflict in which he must define his own existence in order to discover his social function and political culpability: "All of us here are going to know grief; if we live fifty years, we'll have known pain for fifty years. And in the end we'll die. . . . I'm afraid of life! There are times I--I am very frightened. Any happiness seems trivial. . . . It's the self that suffers, and there's a place where the self--ceases."[5] The subtle reverses on the Promethean pattern worked by LeGuin allow this debate to work itself out in Shevak's mind, thus sparing him from the mistake that leads Victor to destruction, Smith to the brink of annihilation, and David to exile.

Why is the Promethean pattern attractive to women science fiction writers? The figure of Prometheus has always been an enigma. The hierarchies of Mediterranean deities did not exist to shower mankind with their beneficence. Their sorties into the mortal world were generally designed to satiate their own physical appetites. The myth of Prometheus is one of those rare classical instances where the lot of mankind is improved by divine interference. At its root, an inferior deity (the Titan or demigod, Prometheus) outwits a supreme deity (Zeus, the patriarch) and thereby advances a lowly and inferior race. The pattern that emerges can be closely identified with the historical situation of woman, who has been forced to assume the status of second-class citizen. If we were to assign sexual valences to the central deities in the myth, Zeus would be masculine and Prometheus feminine. Zeus of course is the supreme patriarch and any challenge to his authority can be interpreted as a victory for woman. There are obvious parallels between the Promethean pattern and some commonly held mis-perceptions about woman. Because he is punished and reduced in potency, Prometheus reflects the misconception that woman was ordained inferior after some primal error on her part. Because he supplants Zeus' authority by wiles instead of strength, he reflects what is widely ascribed as the modus operandi of woman. The notion that Prometheus is a trickster survives from the earliest form of the myth, which was used to explain sacrificial usage. According to the tale, Prometheus attractively wrapped up the entrails of the victim into a fat bundle and closely bound the best parts in a smaller one. Offering Zeus his choice of bundles, the greedy, simple-minded patriarch opted for the fat bundle. Since that time, man has kept the best meat for himself. Woman, it is widely assumed, has to improve her lot similarly, through cunning rather than reason. Prometheus, which means the "forethinker," is also identified with feminine sensibility.

Woman figures further in the Promethean cycle. The epilogue to the tragedy claims that Zeus created woman to confuse man as a kind of retribution for his undeserved gain. The first woman was Pandora who married Prometheus' brother, Epimetheus (the after-thinker), and then let loose all evils into the world from the store-jar where they were kept. Hence, both the provider and the beneficiary were punished. From the feminist perspective, the patriarch Zeus is the ultimate villain in the drama; Prometheus is the interceder and help-mate to man. Very few male deities in classical literature function satisfactorily as feminist models. Prometheus is unique in this respect. He can be viewed as a figure of high moral dignity and as a challenger to patriarchy, positions which would certainly earn him the sympathy of women.

By using the prototype of Prometheus as a model for the male protagonist, the modern woman science fiction writer is able to offer a feminist perspective in a genre built upon excessive sexist stereotyping. The Promethean type demonstrates that man is not invincible, not always right, not completely strong, and not the infallible model of resourcefulness and propriety. It dismantles or demyths the heroic stereotype of the valiant male leader. It reflects the universe as it truly is, as an ongoing tension between discretion and mistake, rather than a simplistic war between good and evil. It shows man as a bumbling interlocuter, and as a delegate, not a powerbroker. The four writers being discussed have created anti-heroes, male protagonists that subvert the prevailing concept of the epic hero. Nearly every accepted trait of the epic hero is challenged, caricatured or reduced through the personalities of the male protagonist in these works. I will specifically examine these authors' treatment of intelligence, motivation and sexuality.

The epic hero is clever and resourceful, but he is not educated or intellectual in the academic sense. Closest to the image of the epic hero among the considered protagonists is Northwest Smith, depicted as a "cautious" man with "good reason behind everything he did." (Moore, pp. 2; 14). To Moore, the heroic image of Northwest Smith is an essential

ingredient of her parody. Ray-guns, dares, "segir" whiskey
and other conventional devices are so obviously linked to
the heroic that the reader quickly catches on to her ironic
intent. In the overtly serious novels examined, the intelligence of the protagonist is an important character trait.
Victor, David and Shevak are all highly educated, intelligent
men with little practical cleverness or resourcefulness.
Their status as educated men is enhanced by contrasts between
childhood and adulthood. The writers make us conscious of
the fact that these males developed intellectually; they are
not detached from the process of growing up and becoming
educated as the epic hero usually appears to be. We see all
three protagonists as youths and watch them progress from
that abstract, unprogrammed status to achieve a high level
of education. Victor Frankenstein first embraces scientific
curiosity as a child: "Curiosity, earnest research to learn
the hidden laws of nature . . . are among the earliest sensations I can remember." (Shelley, p. 36). At the University
of Ingolstadt in upper Bavaria, he studied with a passion
mathematics, chemistry, anatomy and physics. He respected
his teachers and corresponded with eminent scientists. So
too, David Sumner is introduced to the reader as a young boy,
one given to pranks and riotous behavior. However, because
his Uncle Walt, a doctor, did not treat him as a child, David
"decided very early to become a scientist." (Wilhelm, p. 6).
He went to Harvard at the age of seventeen and moved steadily
through the academic rings toward his Ph.D., even attending
Oxford for a year. Finally, we watch young Shevak of Anarres,
a rather demanding and inquisitive youth, amaze his superiors
with his acute perceptions. He is tracked with the best
teachers in the finest institutions of learning. By the age
of twenty-nine, he has already captured the coveted "Seo Sen"
prize in physics. Despite their education and intelligence,
none of these protagonists are clever and resourceful when it
comes to dealing with their work once it escapes the laboratory.
Victor cannot control his monster, nor David his clones, and
Shevak is trapped and manipulated by the socio-political
mechanisms of two worlds. The pattern of the epic hero
collapses in these protagonists. Instead of cleverness and
resourcefulness, traits of the epic hero, we discover highly
trained and intelligent men who are rendered impotent by the
forces of nature and/or culture.

Heroes are motivated by a strong sense of purpose and
serviced by unambiguous talents. The epic hero is a champion;
he is brave, a man of action, successful, devoted to a cause,
loyal to a superior or ideal, and not in the least complex.
The protagonists being discussed do not conform to these
characteristics. All are highly complex individuals, given
to uncertainty, vacillation and indecisiveness. They are not
brave in the accepted masculine sense. Although they embark,
through their work, on fantastic adventures, they each become
frightened by the immensity of the power at their fingertips
and attempt to stop or turn back. Victor and David attempt
to destroy what they have created; Shevak considers never
finishing the theory that he has nearly completed. Although
all of the protagonists "act" in the early stages of their
stories, and thereby generate the cause of their undoing,
they quickly become passive and complacent. Victor cannot

kill his creature, create for it a bride, or stop its fiendish murders. Northwest Smith surrenders his consciousness and will to survive to his shambleau. David sees his authority eclipsed by his creations and is piteously ineffectual in his attempt to destroy the cloning laboratory. Sensing that he is merely a closely monitored pawn, Shevak very nearly disintegrates psychologically, suffering insult with a stoic indifference rather than with aggressive challenge. After losing all of his family, Victor relinquishes his own life while his monster is still loose in the world. Northwest Smith is rescued by his best friend and he can only feebly promise to try to avoid another encounter with a shambleau. David is exiled and the clone community continues to thrive. Shevak does manage to finish his theory and share it with all parties; however, he gains nothing from his work and when we last see him returning to Anarres, "His hands were empty, as they had always been." (LeGuin, p. 311).

Initially, all four protagonists are devoted to a cause, although their motivation can be questioned. Victor's obsession is self-serving; he seems to have given no thought to its application or usefulness to society. Northwest Smith is an outlaw and consequently selfishly serving his own ends. David does owe allegiance to his family, but through his family and their scheme he cuts himself off from the rest of the world. Shevak finds fault with both cultures and pursues an ideal that neither accepts. With the exception of David, who reveres his Uncle Walt, none of the protagonists recognizes a superior. Nor do they pursue a goal that is implicitly good, hence free of the possiblity of evil application. They do not emerge as natural leaders, are not charismatic and do not inspire blind faith in their peers. They are all relatively lonely, isolated individuals condemned to solitude. Victor loses all his loved ones and dies alone in the arctic wastes. Northwest Smith, a scavenger and outlaw, has one friend only, also an outlaw. David watches his relations die off and realizes that there is no common bond between him and his clones; finally he is exiled alone in the wilderness. Shevak is a loner and continuously experiences separation from those few people to whom he is in some way attached: "He was alone, here, because he came from a self-exiled society. He had always been alone on his own world because he had exiled himself from his society." (LeGuin, p. 72). Loneliness and isolation completely displace the sense of community that usually surrounds the epic hero. The pattern of isolation is further complicated by the protagonists' vulnerability, low self-esteem, guilt feelings and obsessions. They all appear to be weak-willed and incapable of protecting themselves. They are obsessed with their initial goals and then by what they perceive as their failures. They do not think highly of themselves and are quick to absorb blame. Although the reader sympathizes with their plights, very little in their behavior is attractive.

The final behavioral category considered is sexuality, and here one discovers the greatest challenge to masculinity and heroism. In the epic hero women are generally a passing fancy and very little treatment is allowed to the theme of sexuality, although by implication heroes are virile, manly and sensually appealing. Among the protagonists being discussed, a great emphasis is placed upon emotional relationships, and sexuality becomes a graphic element of the narratives. Writing under the constraints of nineteenth-century sexual taboos, Mary Shelley could not deal with the sexual theme in an explicit way. However, by suggestion and innuendo, she has created a provocative sexual metaphor. Victor Frankenstein is in love with and engaged to his adopted sister--"the beautiful companion of all my occupations and my pleasures." (Shelley, p. 35). Their love was recognized and condoned by the family and their marriage was long anticipated. Tragically, Victor's monster mars the bliss of their wedding night by slaying Elizabeth in the nuptial chamber in her bed. The murder is a savage parody of the nuptial rite; the fiend supplants Victor in his role of groom, depriving him of his most cherished goal. The subplot of the love affair contains the echoes of two incest themes--a brother-sister relationship, since Victor and Elizabeth were raised together in those roles, and an oedipal relationship, in that the monster (Frankenstein's son) ravages Victor's wife (the mother). Although the presentation of these themes is extremely subtle, the implications are pronounced. Victor, who fails to consummate his marriage, is symbolically emasculated.

The theme of rape is utilized with great imagination in "Shambleau," where the male protagonist is subjected to a reverse rape. Northwest Smith is every inch the macho male provocateur. It is he that shows the first sexual inclination towards the shambleau: "Smith was aware of a stirring excitement within him. . . . He took her by the shoulders . . . dragged her to him . . . sweet yielding brownness in the circle of his arms." (Moore, p. 10). It was only the realization that the shambleau was not quite human that prevented him from following through with a traditional male on female seduction. Later, the shambleau turns the tables and rapes Smith in a graphic sexual parody: "The wet scarlet writhings with moonlight sliding and shining along the thick, worm-round tresses and losing itself in the masses only to glint again and more silvery along writhing tendrils--an awful, shuddering beauty more dreadful than any ugliness could be." (Moore, p. 20). Through alliteration and crisp sexual imagery--blood, worms, writhing, slippery, etc.--the sexual encounter becomes queerly alive and enticing. Moore even manages to capture the ambivalence of the rape victim: "For a moment he went down into a blind abyss of submission; and then somehow the very sight of that obscenity . . . was dreadful enough to draw him out of the seductive darkness." (Moore, p. 19). Depicted as victim instead of assailant, Northwest Smith is also emasculated. The traditional male, patriarchal domain of sexual prowess is challenged by Moore's aggressive and consuming alien feminine avenger.

Kate Wilhelm's treatment of sexuality accurately reflects the shift in roles that is occurring in today's society in which women seek to establish a strong degree of independence. David and Celia are cousins, but have been in love since childhood. Aware of the taboo that forbids inter-family marriages, David and Celia divert their sexual energy into sibling rivalry:

> She pushed him out of the hayloft and broke his arm when he was fifteen, and when he was sixteen they wrestled from the back door of the Wiston farmhouse to the fence, fifty

or sixty yards away. They tore the clothes off each
other, and he was bleeding from her fingernails down his
back, she from scraping her shoulder on a rock. Then
somehow in their rolling and squirming frenzy, his cheek
came down on her uncovered chest, and he stopped fighting.
He suddenly became a melting, sobbing, incoherent idiot
and she hit him on the head with a rock and ended the
fight. (Wilhelm, p. 5).

David and Celia do consummate their relationship, but the
lovers are twice separated. Celia exercises her independent
spirit and desire for self-fulfillment by going off to South
America to train peasant farmers in soil preservation. When
she returns, after a long bout with tropical fever, she is
frail and weak. After a few months of bliss with David, she
dies in his arms. David, permanently frustrated by his loss,
develops a fixation for one of Celia's three clones: "He had
a fantasy in which Celia-3 had come to him shyly and asked
that he take her. In the fantasy he had taken her. . . .
Unable to take it any longer, he had sought out C-3 and asked
her haltingly if she would come to his room with him, and she
had drawn back quickly, involuntarily, with fear written too
clearly on her smooth face." (Wilhelm, p. 40). Separated
from his love, and rejected by his self-created image of his
love, David, too, is emasculated. His sexuality is reduced
to fantasy and his essential manhood is no more than an echo
of his past glory.

Sexuality is given extended treatment in The Dispossessed.
There are graphic treatments of a variety of sexual motifs,
including childbirth, homosexuality and rape. Although
Shevak is "partnered" and has two children, he is twice
separated from his wife. In the first instance, he is
separated by the social planners of his culture, who choose
to delegate him and Takver to separate assignments. Later,
Shevak chooses to go to Urras, thus precipitating another
separation. Despite the positive relationship Shevak has
with his wife, he experiences other relationships, which are
humiliating. His first sexual encounters are less than sat-
isfactory. He has a homosexual encounter with Bedap, both
as an adolescent and later as an adult. But his greatest
sexual humiliation comes on the planet Urras. Shevak develops a fixation for Vea, a married woman, and when he
becomes intoxicated at a party, he makes a clumsy sexual
advance. Vea tries to resist and cautions Shevak to behave,
but he refuses to desist. "He fumbled with one hand at the
complicated clothes he was wearing and managed to get his
trousers unfastened . . . her resistance excited him further.
He gripped her to him, and his semen spurted out against the
white silk of her dress." (LeGuin, p. 185). Dazed Shevak
wanders back into the main room and vomits on a table ladened
with food. Once again, the protagonist is sexually humiliated,
here quite graphically and unequivocally by the early ejacula-
tion, a potent symbol for emasculation. Heroism in all four
protagonists is effectively demythed through metaphors of
sexual inadequacy and emasculation. Deprived of sexual
prowess, the male anti-hero is only a shadow of the traditional male patriarch.

Although these works span 160 years, they are linked by

pattern and intent. Mary Shelley consciously embraces the prototype of Prometheus in her melancholic novel Frankenstein. Three twentieth-century writers have successfully incorporated the same theme in widely acclaimed works. C. L. Moore, Kate Wilhelm and Ursula K. LeGuin are talented writers, each with a unique style and different purpose. However, they each embrace the feminist perspective in the crucial area of the concept of the male protagonist. All four writers have successfully demythed the elevated and bloated stereotype of the epic hero in fiction. They have created ordinary men subject to extraordinary circumstances; the results are to a great extent tragic, but they are honest and realistic. Rather than heroes, they have given us the anti-hero, intelligent rather than clever, complex rather than simple, isolated, guiltridden and vulnerable. They love but they are not great lovers. They try to tamper with the orderly function of the universe and pay a dear price. In terms of intelligence, motivation and sexuality, these writers have introduced a male model that is consistent with a modern feminist perspective that questions the assumptions underlying patriarchal stereotypes. Their design is purposeful, logical and healthy. In so doing, they have moved science fiction one step closer to reality.

Youngstown State University

Notes

[1] C. L. Moore, "Shambleau" in The Best of C. L. Moore (New York: Ballantine, 1975), p. 3. Subsequent references will be listed internally and designated by the author's name.

[2] N. G. L. Hammond, ed., The Oxford Classical Dictionary (London: Oxford University Press, 1970), p. 883. All references to the Prometheus myth are taken from the OCD.

[3] Mary Wollstonecraft Shelley, Frankenstein, or the Modern Prometheus (London: Oxford University Press, 1969), p. 101.

[4] Kate Wilhelm, Where Late The Sweet Birds Sang (New York: Harper & Row, 1976), pp. 39; 44.

[5] Ursula K. LeGuin, The Dispossessed (New York: Avon, 1974), p. 48.

Kathe Davis Finney

The Days of Future Past
or
Utopians Lessing and LeGuin Fight Future Nostalgia

The writer who wants to create a genuinely helpful, realistic Utopia has a basic problem. Doris Lessing and Ursula LeGuin are two such writers. They have come from opposite directions. Lessing moves from mainstream realism (Robert Scholes calls her "a classic example of the autobiographical realist who must wait between each book in order to live through enough material to fuel the next one[1]); LeGuin moves from science fiction to similar concerns, thoughts, forms. I'd like to look at two novels by each author: LeGuin's best-known work, The Left Hand of Darkness, and the more explicitly Utopian The Dispossessed, and the first two of Lessing's new series Canopus in Argos: Archives: Shikasta and The Marriages Between Zones Three, Four, and Five. The juxtaposition makes clear how much the two women are engaged in the same enterprise, and also clarifies that enterprise.

Lessing's present work is a continuation of the close and accurate observation for which her admirers have rightly praised her, and from which they wrongly supposed the science fiction to be a deviation. LeGuin's work is likewise powerful partly because it is strong in those feature in which science fiction is characteristically weak. As utopias then, they're anomalous. Utopias are anti-realistic. As Scholes points out, for the last couple of centuries we have been in the habit of dividing narrative into "two great schools of fiction according to the relationship between the fictional worlds they present and the world of human experience."[2] Realistic fiction (the novel) presents a recognizable version of that world. Fantasy, with other forms of romance, "always insists upon a radical discontinuity between its world and the world of ordinary human experience."[3] (In this scheme it's easy to see why debate can continue to rage over the status of science fiction, which began in romance and has that root affinity with fantasy, yet has moved in many cases so completely into modes we call realistic.)

Utopias are a species of romance. By definition they present a country or world that is not our own--"nowhere"--and a set of experiences that counters rather than copies ours. They do so in order to make a point about our world, of course. Like "allegory, satire, fable, parable, and so on," utopias are a variety of what Scholes calls didactic romance or fabulation, romance which "yet returns to confront that known world in some cognitive way."[4] This confrontation is an indirect one however. Utopia points up the defects of our actual condition by illustrating alternatives, but our reality's failures are mostly just implicit in the contrast. The utopian form remains as profoundly conventional as Northrop Frye points out all romance is.[5] Whatever the surface realism in the presentation of everyday life in utopia, the fictional forms will be as fixedly structured and the rules as rigid as those of a chess game.

Michael Holquist develops the chess comparison convincingly and at length in "How to Play Utopia: . . ."

> Baldly stated, my thesis is that the relationship of chess to battle is roughly parallel to the relationship which obtains between utopia and actual society.[6]

The gamelike qualities of utopia are its simplification and abstraction, its "radical stylization of something which in experience is of enormous complexity . . ." and its rule-governed nature: "The chess game has rules, the utopia laws." (p. 135, Holquist's emphasis).

Anyone who fails to understand this fundamental nature of utopias, who tries to take the model literally (to read romance as novel), will look for the wrong things, says Holquist:

> When critics complain that there are no great utopias they usually mean that there are no utopias which contain plots or characters of the depth and complexity found in more conventional works of fiction. This is to miss the point completely, to complain that chess is inferior because it lacks the body contact of football. (p. 136).

But for Lessing and LeGuin the problem is not in how the model is taken, but in the model itself--or in the very fact of its being a model. Chess and football, different as they are, both are still games. Lessing and LeGuin wish to escape or transcend, not merely particular conventions, but utopian conventionality itself. Toward that end they reject much of what would seem most necessarily and essentially utopian, without giving up the utopian project.

In its conventionality, the traditional utopia fails with respect to the future the same way that nostalgia fails with respect to the past. Nostalgia is that sentiment derived from looking back to a past time as ideal, a Golden Age or sunny childhood or peak experience after which present experience seems degenerate. The enormously superior state

of affairs which we are always capable of imagining may be
objectified and given a hypothetical existence in either
the past or the future; it doesn't really matter which,
since both are mythic, outside actual time. Paradisal past
is of a kind with utopian future, Eden just one more utopia.
Utopia merely aims its nostalgia in the other temporal
direction: it offers future nostalgia.

Etymologically, nostalgia is the pain of longing for the
return home; homesickness. The problem is that the sentiment is inherently false. Lessing, as early as her Children
of Violence series, was protesting what she called "the
dishonesty of nostalgia." The dishonesty there lies in the
fact that the childhood perfection remembered was not perfection when it was lived. But the point is that even had it
been somehow truly perfect, it could not be returned to.
The nature of time and process insures that we can't go
home again. Since nostalgia is the longing for what in
the nature of time itself is impossible, it is illegitimate.
Such a longing is a denial of lived reality. That is why
Lessing, in Memoirs of a Survivor, calls nostalgia "the
craving, the regret . . . that poisoned itch." Insofar as
utopias simply cater to that craving, they too are illegitimate.

The imagination of perfection is of course not what is
objectionable. Such imagining is how we give form and
meaning to our lives. Northrop Frye says:

> The imaginative vision of human life sees it as a drama
> in four acts: a fall [from a paradise or now-lost
> world], the struggle of men in a fallen world which is
> what we usually think of as history, the world's redemp-
> tion . . . and an apocalypse.[7]

In that scheme, utopias are visions of redemption, or of the
perfection precipitated by apocalypse. (And modern science
fiction utopias tend to be messianically motivated, though
their scientific trappings and style of tough realism might
disguise that fact.) "Imaginative vision" means experience
shaped as the imagination would have it: paradise is a
projection of human desire. We transfer that story to our
individual lives to give them meaning too.[8] But desire is
famous for misleading us. By Shikasta Lessing has made
nostalgia the very air of the purgatorial Zone Six, which

> can present to the unprepared every sort of check, delay
> and exhaustion. This is because the nature of this
> place is a strong emotion--"nostalgia" is their word
> for it--which means a longing for what has never been,
> or at least not in the form and shape imagined. (pp. 5-6).

LeGuin doesn't use the term nostalgia, but her point about
pleasure (as opposed to fulfillment) is essentially the same
one:

> The search for pleasure is circular, repetitive, atemporal.
> . . . It has an end. It comes to the end and has to
> start over. It is not a journey and return, but a
> closed cycle, a locked room, a cell. (The Dispossessed,

p. 268).

Perfection is static. It is atemporal because it cannot admit of change, since; once perfection has been achieved, no change can be an improvement. That's why "society ceases to be a live organism in the utopia." But we live in time, in change, contingency and process. So real society _is_ a live organism, and Lessing and LeGuin want to incorporate that reality in their utopia. That process which would seem to be the antithesis of utopia is for these two writers the essence of it: "Fulfillment . . . is a function of time," says LeGuin. (The Dispossessed, p. 268). They present imperfect utopias therefore, worlds not fully achieved. These worlds not only are in process, they quite evidently always will be. There is no more telos than nostos. Or rather, homecoming and aim are radically reconceived. There is no end beyond life itself: "There was process: process was all." (The Dispossessed, p. 268). The human significance of process, the sense of being at home in the universe, can only be found in an acceptance of process, what George Kearns calls "nostos without nostalgia."[9] Each of these four novels presents "An Ambiguous Utopia," as LeGuin subtitles The Dispossessed. And each utopia is ambiguous in more ways than one.

The typical utopia accomplishes its comment on our own society by means of contrast. As Holquist points out, the usual pattern is one of journey from the familiar society to the utopia and then return home. Lessing and LeGuin both use the pattern of voyage and return, but alter it. In none of these four novels is the journey from home to utopia and back again. The change in the pattern points up not just the ambiguities of the utopias, but ultimately the ambiguity of the very idea of utopia.

The Left Hand of Darkness and Shikasta have a surprising (even a suspicious) number of similarities. In both, a galactic federation is trying benevolently to affect the course of events on the planet which is the focus of attention, a planet in an important state of transition; and the attempt is primarily through one agent, who becomes our main channel of information, who often, through his reports, is our narrator. In both cases then he is traveling _from_ the higher, if not ideal, world to the benighted one.

In Shikasta Johor is emissary to the familiar world, for the fallen Shikasta is very recognizably our own planet. The reverse direction of the voyage might be explained by viewing Shikasta as a reverse utopia, but this dystopia also has a utopia within it. (Shikasta could be said to be utopian at both ends.) The planet has begun as Rohanda, a garden world recognizable as paradise with its helpful communicating plants and animals, and "no division between the physical and mental." (p. 32). In this Edenic state an evolving mankind has lived in happy symbiosis with a more highly evolved race, the "giants of the earth" of the Bible and legend. Thrown out of cosmic harmony by a disaster, an unforeseen disruption in the pattern of the stars, Rohanda becomes Shikasta, "the hurt one." The novel charts its history, our own, into the near future and near holocaust. The novel ends with the suggestion of a superior world to come. As the old civilization breaks down, a new breed of children is being trained in a new kind of group life. Planetary balance will be restored; paradise will be regained. But Lessing, even with her apparent acceptance of what LeGuin calls the "Velikovsky-von Daniken school of, as it were, thought," explicitly rejects the idea of rescue, and has Johor recognize and reject his desire to respond as a child to the great figures' parental authority and power of reassurance.

Though the world of The Left Hand of Darkness' envoy, Genly Ai, is also our own, it has been assimilated into the more-or-less Utopian Hainish Ekumen. The planet he visits, Gethen, is likewise ambiguous as a utopia; certainly it is no garden, with its unrelenting ice-age climate. Still, it casts the light of contrast on Ai's views, Hainishly enlightened as those already are, and particularly offers alternatives to earthly dichotomies.

Most notable is the Gethenian freedom from sex difference. While that is biologically determined and therefore scarcely available to us, the gender-free attitudes and practices it produces are somewhat more applicable. War is unknown. The reader's first view of the Gethenians is in a parade, but "They do not march in step. This is a parade with no soldiers, not even imitation soldiers." (p. 8). The dominance of technology has been limited somewhat by the climate, and the technology quietly present is not alienating. Even in summer trucks can go little faster than a person walking, and cities are designed to accommodate the cold and snow rather than to deny or simply overcome it. There is a greater continuity with the past (which is paradoxically what makes possible the fact that "It is always the Year One here." (p. 8). And the "primitive" harmony of the natural world and the universe are understood as sacred.

In Lessing's Marriages, it is again the superior civilization, in this case very utopian, which sends its representative, indeed its leader, to the lower Zone (not our world, though manifesting some of its failures). She is a queen, Al'Ith, complete with castle and flowing gown, though her realm is free of hierarchy, weapons, and other paraphernalia of the usual medievalistic romance world. Zone Three is an idyllic paradise of natural harmony (enough so that one was dubbed his review "Al'Ith in Wonderland"). Yet this is the world that gets its comeuppance by exposure to another.

Part of the effect of these reversals of the usual pattern is to call into question the superiority of supposed utopias, and beyond that to undermine our assumptions about perfection, including and especially its fixity. The question of what the ideal ought to be is raised explicitly in The Dispossessed, in which the same reversal occurs, with Shevek journeying from his utopian world Anarres to the corrupt mother world Urras and home again. His home is a near-desert world, with few varieties of plants and fewer of animals, sparse natural resources and sparser creature comforts. If that weren't formidably austere enough, the society is a true anarchy, with not only no government, but also no money, no private property, no nuclear families. But Shevek, never having doubted its fundamental rightness, is not prepared to be overwhelmed by the beauty of the despised decedent "propertarian" Urras:

> It was the most beautiful view Shevek had ever seen.
> The tenderness and vitality of the colors, the mixture
> of rectilinear human design and powerful, proliferate
> natural contours, the variety and harmony of the elements,
> gave an impression of complex wholeness such as he had
> never seen, except, perhaps, foreshadowed on a small
> scale in certain serene and thoughtful human faces. . . .
> This is what a world is supposed to look like, Shevek
> thought. (p. 52).

And again, "he did feel at home. He could not help it."
(p. 62). So we're confronted with the question of just what
is ideal and, like Shevek, are forced to consider the possibility that our notion of perfection may itself be flawed.

In conventional utopias, the exposure to an ideal society
permits or forces the voyager (and the reader) to see and
acknowledge the failures of his own society, which, without
such exposure, the normal well-adjusted citizen is likely to
have taken for granted. Anthropology, by confronting us with
other cultures, likewise forces the realization that our most
cherished assumptions, those held so closely that we are not
even aware of them as assumptions, are not necessary or
universally shared.

Holquist assumes that the utopian author, unlike his main
character, already knows what the ideal is:

> The utopian impulse . . . can be said to have its source
> in a distinctive anthropology: the utopist, before he
> writes a line, begins by postulating what the best man
> would be. (p. 144).

and then postulates the society which would produce such a
person. But in that case the voyager's assumptions are merely
replaced by the utopists'. Both Lessing and LeGuin are interested in producing a more fundamental anthropological
relativism. LeGuin, famously the child of anthropologists and
herself trained in the field, deploys the whole arsenal of
anthropological techniques in her fiction. That she uses
the methodology to create cultures rather than to investigate
existing ones doesn't mean that she thinks she has the
answers, or even believes that there are answers, in any
final sense. Science fiction is a suitable medium for her
not only because it permits her a cosmic rather than just an
earthly transcultural perspective, but also because science
fiction has always specialized in the alien, with the self-expansion involved in the effort at comprehension.

Like _The Left Hand of Darkness_, Lessing's _Shikasta_ is
composed entirely of "documents," field notes, interviews,
excerpts from official histories, and so on. The intent too
is like LeGuin's, I think: to offer for interpretation a
body of foreign "data" which itself challenges what one might
have begun by thinking was "the best," to maintain an
attitude of open questioning rather than to replace one
set of closed convictions with another.

The loss of deeply-held convictions is not only personally
unnerving, it sets one apart from one's fellows. Utopian
voyagers have always served, willy-nilly, as anthropological
reporters in some sense, and have always paid for their insight into a different world with alienation from their own.

When Genly Ai sees single-sexed people again, they seem as strange and repugnant to him as humans did to Gulliver after life among the Houyhnhnms.

The ambassador/investigator thus easily becomes a sacrificial figure, giving his happiness or his life for the merging of two cultures and the enlightenment of his own. Heinlein's Michael Valentine Smith is the most obviously Christ-like example in science fiction. Johor is the only one of these envoys actually to die (unless you count Estraven as Ai's alter ego), but all four suffer in various and deeply personal ways for their role.

For both Lessing and LeGuin, the process by which one arrives at fulfillment involves suffering and pain; and the process itself is essential to the fulfillment. There are no shortcuts. Shevek realizes:

> It was joy they were both after--the completeness of being. If you evade suffering you also evade the chance of joy. Pleasure you may get, or pleasures, but you will not be fulfilled. You will not know what it is to come home. (p. 268).

But the passage through suffering, though necessary and inevitable, does not bring us to an end, a conclusion, a stoppage of time. The process that brings us to "redemption" does so by making clear that process is all there is. "Home" is in the knowledge and acceptance.

Social failure may lie then simply in the failure to recognize the need for change. Shevek's society "was conceived as a permanent revolution." (p. 267). His trip away from it is prompted by the recognition that revolution, which "begins in the thinking mind," has ossified into rules which are no less binding for being unwritten. His friend Bedap rants against "Public opinion! . . . the unadmitted, inadmissible government that rules the Odonian society by stifling the individual mind." (p. 134). So Shevek leaves to make a pathway for change and exchange, an opening.

Lessing's pastoral Zone Three is likewise becalmed, though the people have not been aware of it until, significantly, healthy births cease. This very complacency is the problem: "We did think . . . of ourselves in interaction with these other realms, but it was in an abstract way. We had perhaps grown insular? Self-sufficing?" (p. 6). Al·Ith's visits, like Shevek's, produce revolutionary activity and radical change, with the pain and risk necessarily involved. But the result is the restoration, not of perfection, which is static, but of the openness that is life:

> There was a continuous movement now, . . . There was a lightness, a freshness, and an enquiry and a remaking and an inspiration where there had been only stagnation. And closed frontiers. . . . The movement is not all one way-- not by any means. (p. 245).

Holquist says "utopias have laws," but laws represent a fixity that is inimical to the spirit of what both these writers consider utopia; and so their worlds, insofar as they are utopian, are singularly lawless. Anarres is absolutely so; Zone Three operates in harmony with a cosmic Order, but by means of "inner listening." (p. 55). There is no compulsion (and hence no guilt), and the people are horrified at its existence in the lower Zones. Shikasta ends with a post-calamity hopefulness that is marked by the cessation of compulsory rule:

> I was taking it absolutely for granted, but absolutely, that there were going to be different factions and the rulers and the armies and the police and I would have to watch my step and be careful what I said. . . . But after a couple of days I felt a great relax all over my body, like yawning and stretching, and then I suddenly understood I wasn't afraid of doing the wrong thing and landing in prison or ending up as butchers' meat. (p. 359).

Out of this freedom emerges the beauty of a city constructed in harmony with larger principles of order: "It is the most beautiful place I can remember. Again, no one knows anything about plans or architects, it just grew up, or so it would seem." (p. 359).

The conviction of the complex balance of forces in the universe pervades LeGuin's work, as everyone has noticed, and as the title of The Left Hand of Darkness expresses. Lessing shares essentially the same vision. Both emphasize that this is a dynamic balance. Shikasta is an extreme instance: "This planet is above all one of contrasts and contradictions, because of its in-built stresses. Tension is its essential nature. This is its strength. This is its weakness." (p. 5). But she also says something similar about the entire universe:

> This is a catastrophic universe, always; and subject to sudden reversals, upheavals, changes, cataclysms, with joy never anything but the song of substance under pressure forced into new forms and shapes. (p. 3).

Not surprisingly, such a vision of unity in opposition produces an imagery and a use of paradox which link Lessing and LeGuin to such poets as Blake as well as to a visionary religious tradition.

Our whole mythic tradition tells us that the only return is forward. Homer, the Gospels, Dante, all show that the ascent, the way to salvation or the way home, begins with the descent, with a confrontation with death or hell or some other form of ultimate fallenness. Lessing and LeGuin are both deeply aware of that tradition and use it richly; it appears in the form as well as the substance of their work. Lessing explains in the preface to Shikasta how the science fiction genre filled her with "the exhilaration that comes from being set free into a larger scope"; this freedom, she says, is

> to be as experimental as I like, and as traditional: the next volume in this series, The Marriages . . . , has turned out to be a fable, or myth. Also, oddly enough, to be more realistic.

She is realistic, like LeGuin, in order that the fictions not be dismissed as romance, mere wish-fulfillment. Both authors attempt to satisfy, without betraying us, as nostalgia does, the need nostalgia expresses. They would insert the shapes of fulfilled desire into reality. But they can do so only by offering a different vision of fulfillment, one that can accommodate reality. Bedap tells Shevek:

> What drives people crazy is trying to live outside reality. Reality is terrible. It can kill you. Given time it certainly will kill you. The reality is pain-- you said that! But it's the lies, the evasions of reality, that drive you crazy. (p. 134).

The future nostalgia of utopias is an evasion of reality. Lessing and LeGuin know perfectly well that utopias are conventional, but they want to change the conventions without giving up utopia. They want their chess to have body contact. They want a game of chess played by the pieces on the board, with the rules changing as they go. That is, after all, how we live. "You can go home again," says LeGuin, "so long as you understand that home is a place where you have never been." I would like to conclude by quoting that entire passage.

> You shall not go down twice to the same river, nor can you go home again. That he knew; indeed it was the basis of his view of the world. Yet from that acceptance of transience he evolved his vast theory, wherein what is most changeable is shown to be fullest of eternity, and your relationship to the river, and the river's relationship to you and to itself, turns out to be at once more complex and more reassuring than a mere lack of identity. You can go home again, the General Temporal Theory asserts, so long as you understand that home is a place where you have never been.

Kent State University

Notes

[1] *Structural Fabulation* (New York: Oxford University Press, 1979), p. 23.

[2] *Structural Fabulation*, p. 28.

[3] Ibid.

[4] *Structural Fabulation*, p. 29

[5] Throughout his book-length study of the subject, *The Secular Scripture: A Study of the Structure of Romance* (Cambridge, Mass.: Harvard University Press, 1976).

[6] "How to Play Utopia: Some Brief Notes on the Distinctiveness of Science Fiction. *Science Fiction: A Collection of Critical Essays*, ed. Mark Rose (Englewood Cliffs: Prentice Hall, 1976), pp. 132-146.

[7] *Fearful Symmetry: A Study of William Blake* (Princeton: Princeton University Press, 1947; paper ed. 1969), p. 357.

⁸I am thinking of Frank Kermode's discussion of this matter in The Sense of an Ending: Studies in the Theory of Fiction (New York: Oxford University Press, 1967), where he speaks of "a permanent need to live by the pattern rather than the fact." (p. 11).

⁹Guide to Ezra Pound's Selected Cantos (New Brunswick: Rutgers University Press, 1980), p. 23.

Mary T. Brizzi

Narcissism and Romance in McCaffrey's Restoree

Anne McCaffrey's Restoree is unique among science fiction novels. McCaffrey's critics are quick to attack the shallow histrionics of characterization, the Harlequin Romance stereotypes, the improbable reactions of heroes and villains alike, the inconsistencies of plot, and the saccharine posturings of the melodramatic heroine, Sara.[1] McCaffrey herself waves aside these attacks:

> No one had told me that women were not supposed to write [science fiction] and that few read it. After seven years of voracious reading in the field, I'd had it up to the eyeteeth with vapid women. I rebelled. I wrote Restoree as a tongue-in-cheek protest, utilizing as many of the standard "thud and blunder" cliches as possible. . . . few male readers tumbled to the fact that I had deliberately written a space gothic.[2]

Undeniably, the book, read as parody, is funny. Perhaps Restoree really is the voice of the feminist fan. Yet few reviewers took it as a joke, nor, I suggest, did many readers. It was accepted for publication and printed without being identified as a spoof (as mass-market spoofs like Bored of the Rings generally are): it is still in print in an edition that does not suggest National Lampoon treatment of either the gothic or science fiction elements. I suggest that the appeal of the novel, far from humor, is a relentless exploitation of powerful romantic fantasies that, regardless of their degrading narcissism, strike at the heart of women's erotic imagery in our civilization. More, I would say the novel is a sharper, more condensed setting forth of these images, prefiguring much of the eroticism in McCaffrey's later, more subtle work.

I am tempted to reduce these images and fantasies to a fairy-tale portrait gallery, and most particularly to the

Cinderella motif. But I think they are more trenchant than mere fairy tales, and it is our recognition of their pervasive effect in our erotic view of women's lives that gives McCaffrey's characterizations their validity. Not that I am agreeing with McCaffrey that her trump card is characterization; I have always held that her greater gift is density of speculative and scientific ideas. She abases her characters with these narcissistic erotic images; she raises them up again with their confrontations with dragon, crystal, cyborgs, extrasensory perception. Lessa being fed by F'lar and admired as "almost pretty," or deliberately irritating his knife wounds, is an empty social butterfly; Lessa impressing Ramoth the Golden inspires the reader with a true Sense of Wonder.

But it is difficult to separate these erotic images from the fairy-tale world, so I'll use the language of fairy-tales to describe them. All of them are narcissistic; all of them presuppose that fragile beauty is a woman's primary tool in dealing with life's problems. I call these images: the Cinderella-butterfly; the pearl before swine; the uncritically adored beloved beautiful even with a dirty face; the vulnerable frail whose act of heroism culminates as she collapses in her adoring lover's arms; and the mutilatee.

The Cinderella motif pervades McCaffrey's work. Throughout, poor, industrious, pretty girls become miraculously rich through the graces of a dashing benefactor; wicked stepmothers and sisters denigrate their beauty and virtue; homely slugs metamorphize into lovely butterflies. McCaffrey's women even show a predilection for losing their shoes while running toward or away from their swains. In Restoree, the homely Sara Fulton was born with natural deformities to which nurture has added its graceless two cents' worth: a big nose, a predisposition to obesity, corns, and even hairy arms. The family drudge, she wastes her girlhood cooking and ironing for an ungrateful batch of brothers. However, like Cinderella, she is hard working and escapes the grinding poverty of her home town in the razzle-dazzle of New York. In other words, Cinderella goes to the ball.

The fairy godmother takes an unlikely form, however. Captured by "cellular giants," aliens who butcher sentients for meat (there is no explanation of their predilection for sentient meat, a sly touch of humor on McCaffrey's part), she is cut up into pieces. However, a mad scientist, Monsorlit, from the planet Lothar gets hold of these pieces somehow, and "restores" her to life, improving her appearance even to the extent of giving her a natural suntan. Unfortunately, this treatment is highly illegal since it makes all its beneficiaries into zombies. So she is drafted to serve as attendant in a mental institution. There she meets her Prince Charming, Harlan, a member of the Lotharian royal family. Unfortunately, Harlan has been drugged ga-ga by his enemies. Sara rescues him and spends the remainder of the book in political intrigues and wars which restore him to his rightful position. He falls in love with Sara early in the book, without trying to ascertain whether Lotharians can interbreed with Earthlings, though they certainly do try.

Sara Fulton is only the most blatant of McCaffrey's Cinderella figures. Lessa, of the Pern novels, first appears in Dragonflight as a repulsive drudge. F'lar, her Prince

Charming, appears before her transformation; but the scene in which she bathes and washes her hair revealing concealed loveliness echoes Cinderella's magic transformation, and with a sensuality appropriate to the contemporary gothic romance. Lessa's true fairy godmother is her dragon Ramoth for when Lessa bonds with Ramoth she becomes Weyrwoman and partner to the political and military leader of Weyr society, the Weyrleader. In fact, it is her sexual alliance with him that confers power, just as Cinderella's sexual attractiveness obtains for her a royal alliance.

Again in the Pern series, Menolly goes from rags to, if not riches, at least her heart's desire, when she is rescued by a handsome dragonrider (she has just lost her shoes, by the way), and brought to the palace-like Harper Hall. Other facets of the Cinderella story appear in "Cinderella Switch" in Judy-Lynn del Rey's Stellar 6, where a mysterious lady engineer, thought to be a street commoner, arrays herself in a magic field of light, calculated to fade at midnight. Though Dacia is already a person of consequence, she does meet a charming prince, and lose her slipper, at a fancy dress ball. And as with Cinderella, her beauty and finery, not her ability as an engineer, prove her trump cards.

A poor girl's discovery of her own latent extranormal mental powers, in "Apple," lends itself only to a childish desire for adornment. In fact, Maggie O gives herself away by stealing shoes to go with her stolen finery, like Cinderella's slippers again. Though the tale ends tragically, still Maggie O is an ironic Cinderella, who is suddenly released from poverty into a world of glamor by a magic gift--psi talent. Again narcissism governs feminine characterization.

Heroines in McCaffrey's mystery-romance novels, Ring of Fear, Mark of Merlin, and The Kilternan Legacy, likewise experience elevation in socioeconomic level as a result of the impact of their attractiveness, wholesome and innocent though it may be, to men. Of course, this is less surprising than finding the same motif in McCaffrey's science fiction novels.

Cinderella lives in a world of wicked, ugly stepsisters, swine before whom her pearls of grace, charm, sweetness, and wholesome sexual appeal are cast. In Restoree, these stepsisters take the form of Kalina and Cherez, whom Sara encounters as she parades around in her Cinderella-like ballgown at the palace Eclipse party. These two court ladies are just plain vulgar, with their wanton airs and heavy makeup. But Sara's catty streak really has full scope with Harlan's perfidious former mistress, Maritha. The fact that Maritha may have poisoned Harlan is nowhere near as damning as the fact that she notices that Sara is prettier than she is and threatens to have her ejected from the palace. Maritha's insecure reliance on her physical charm damns her even as Sara's similar dependency leads to success. Wicked stepsister is but the dark mirror image of Cinderella.

Maritha is by no means the only swinish wicked stepsister in McCaffrey's work. Rather she is an early prototype, remarkable for her brazen vanity. Such characters as the untidily fickle Kylara in the dragon series show that love of one's own person is truly damning, if one is cast as

the villainess. Kylara is the dragonrider whose infidelities
and vanity cause the death of Brekke's dragon. In fact,
Kylara saves her figure from the ravages of childbearing
though early abortion caused by staying between too long.
Lessa somehow doesn't have these problems keeping her figure.
Nor does Lessa's dragon go into a mating cycle at inconvenient times. Kylara, cynical, vain, and insecure, is a
true wicked stepsister.

Menolly, in Dragonsinger, is beset by swine, too: Holder's
daughters who are ignorant and rude and who challenge her
right to buy a pretty belt for adornment. In The Ship Who
Sang, Helva is forced to endure Ansra Colmer, a malicious,
preening, even murderous actress. But again, Ansra's villainy
shows up in her narcissism, her desire to play a theatrical
role and deny applause to others. Helva is almost her mirror
image, for Helva decides that she too wants the self-aggrandizing pleasures of the state.

Killashandra, the vain, bitchy, insecure heroine of
Crystal Singer, is a unique case because she melds qualities
of Cinderella and the wicked stepsister. In this mature
work, McCaffrey seems finally to recognize the common thread
of narcissism that runs through both types of character, and
finally to integrate them in one fascinating heroine.

Related to the Cinderella myth again is the adoring swain,
the lover whose uncritical adulation of the heroine would in
real life border on pathology. Harlan, in Restoree, is a
recognizable stereotype from the gothic romance. His rugged
good looks and penetrating gaze reveal his sterling character
and, of course, his power to confer riches and happiness on
Sara, his Cinderella. He has a fatal flaw--at the beginning
of the book he is stark raving mad. But the minute he lays
sane eyes on Sara, he falls violently in love even though
she is a mental patient, possibly a Frankensteinlike restoree,
and an alien to boot. His habit of calling her "my dear
lady" rather bothers her, and it bothers her worse when she
finds out that it is the equivalent of a wedding vow on this
quaint planet.

We can well believe that McCaffrey intends this dashing
figure to be something of a parody. His name sounds like
"Harlequin," as in the romances of the same name. As a random
example of this stock figure from gothic romance, we could
cite Rafe in McCaffrey's own mystery-romance, Ring of Fear.
His annoying verbal tic is calling Nialla "dear heart" while
showering every kind of treasure on her, with very little
motivation and less caution about her mysterious background.

But uncritical love, often linked with male nurturance and
almost magical removal of all the heroine's problems, is a
common theme in McCaffrey's science fiction. Thus it is with
Henry Darrow and Molly Mahoney in To Ride Pegasus. Even where
irrational love at first sight is not invoked, males are often
shown as more nurturant than we expect in real life. F'lar
is shown feeding bits of meat to Lessa after rescuing her from
Ruatha. F'nor ministers in an almost motherly fashion to
Brekke after she becomes catatonic because of her dragon's
death.

In Cinderella stories, this uncritical love is unmotivated;
but in McCaffrey's work there is a pattern of motivation. The
Cinderella figure often carries out some act of daring and
courage, after which her frail nature betrays her so she can

collapse into her lover's nurturant arms. Hence Sara in
Restoree rescues Harlan, teaches him to sail a boat though
she hardly knows how herself, swims, walks, and runs with
him to safety--and then collapses into his arms (and into
his bed, though innocently). At intervals she is fed or has
her wounds attended to by him. (There is an enormous amount
of feeding as a method of showing love in McCaffrey's work,
from feeding of hatchling dragons and fire lizards to the
feeding of lovers. But that is another topic.) It is almost
as if McCaffrey is parodying her own mystery-romance novels,
as where Nialla in Ring of Fire rescues a horse from a fiery
barn and then falls exhausted into her lover's arms, or
where the heroine in The Mark of Merlin is liquored into
insensibility by Major Laird after her harrowing journey.

But the pattern of heroism and falling into a lover's
arms is not confined to Restoree and the mystery-romances.
In Dragonflight, Lessa makes a courageous trip through time
to bring dragonriders forward. On her return, she waits for
F'lar, motionless, weeping. And it is when F'lar embraces
her after this flight that they become entirely emotionally
bonded.

Though Helva, a cyborg and the heroine of The Ship Who Sang,
cannot be comforted with food, liquor, or even a cozy bed after
her harrowing adventure with the Xixon, she is given a sort of
loverly comfort by Niall Parollan, who shows concern and even
sighs in relief when she proves hale after this horrible
experience.

In Dragonsong, Menolly is rescued after her historic and
recordbreaking discovery of fire lizards and her brush with
the menace of Thread, though T'gran, the dragonrider who
rescues her, treats her wounds, and offers her analgesic
drink, is not actually her lover. Master Robinton, who
rescues her in a more subtle way by restoring her music to
her, takes on more lover-like overtones. Thus the pattern
of adventure, rescue, and collapse into the nurturant lover's
arms exists throughout McCaffrey's work.

The value of beauty and physical perfection is most strongly emphasized in McCaffrey's work, however, by the motif of
mutilation, amputation, and deformity. Beyond the superficial
Freudian significance of this motif, the meaning of deformity
varies richly in these works but demonstrates a sharp aware-
ness of the extent to which a woman's value and self-image
is determined by her physical appearance. In Restoree, the
pattern is almost fairy-tale-like. Sara is born ugly,
mutilated by aliens, and restored to beauty. On earth,
before her mutilation or restoration, she is unable to obtain
love. After she is given physical beauty, she gains not just
love but power and prestige as well.

Menolly's mutilated hand, though it does not reflect
simple sexual allure, prevents her from seeking adulation
from an admiring audience who might listen to her music.
Thus her musical ability is a tool of her narcissism. Her
happiness is restored only when the hand regains its
flexibility.

Some forms of deformity or mutilation are compensated by
other talents. For example, Helva's birth defects are compensated when she is allowed to become the brain of a powerful ship. And she is able to participate in a limited way

in the life of "mobiles." Through telepathy and the Corvikian envelopes she obtains knowledge of odors and tastes, and even sex. Though her relationship with her passenger or "brawn" is primarily non-sexual, it is a type of love relationship as her bereavement over Jennan and her delight with Niall demonstrates.

Killashandra, in Crystal Singer, suffers a more subtle form of deformity. Her voice, she learns after years of training, has a defect that will prevent her from ever becoming a truly great performer. Her compensation is that she can mine crystal and become wealthy through her musical talents. Again, the voice is a kind of auditory manifestation of physical beauty, so that its defect is a failure of sexual allure and personal display. In this mature work, McCaffrey explores the emptiness of such extraordinary talent because Killashandra's wealth becomes useless as crystal destroys her memory.

This interest in loss, deformity, defect, or amputation goes beyond the reliance of a Cinderella figure on sexual charm to obtain love and power. The mentally retarded empath, Orley, in "Apple," the dwarfed and neuter dragon Ruth in The White Dragon, Lytol and Brekke, the man and woman who have lost their dragons, all these are examples of McCaffrey's later and more mature exploration of this theme of loss and deformity that was first stated in Restoree.

Restoree is critically interesting that it explores these images of allure, beauty, sexual display, and their opposites in ways that show their profound impact on feminine psychology. The works themselves are neither feminist nor sexist. All they do is demonstrate the power of certain erotic fantasies, fairy tales if you will, in our civilization. Cinderella, the charming prince, the ugly stepsister, the frail adventuress, the ugly duckling are inescapable images to most of us. Insofar as we identify with them, evoke them in subconscious fantasies or literary works, or even rebel against them, they draw us and excite us as meaningful, even irritating images in a work of literature. Restoree is not McCaffrey's best book, but its almost naive representation of themes she later elaborates so richly in more mature work gives it a vivid appeal and illuminates her later characterizations.

Kent State University

Notes

[1] See for example Margo Skinner's review in Fantastic, 18:3 (Feb. 1969), 144, or Marion Zimmer Bradley's review in Delap's F & SF Review (March-April 1978), 35.

[2] Anne McCaffrey, "Romance and Glamour in Science Fiction," in: Science Fiction Today and Tomorrow, ed. Reginald Bretnor (New York: Harper & Row, 1974), p. 282.

David L. Foster

Woman on the Edge of Narrative:
Language in Marge Piercy's Utopia

Joanna Russ, in "What Can a Heroine Do; or Why Women Can't Write," has stated that most plots employed by mundane fiction and science fiction don't work for women.[1] Certainly, much recent science fiction has tried to find new ways of telling stories, and it is the assumption of this paper that many fans and writers, and all feminists, would like to see the genre continue to evolve. Particularly, utopian literature by women writers has tried to construct cultures that question the male "monomyth"--defined by Jewett and Lawrence as a story where an edenic society is rescued from evil by a selfless, celibate hero, who, often by means of sexual renunciation, triumphs and then recedes.[2] Essays by Carol Pearson and Russ, both of which appear in Marleen Barr's Future Females, outline some common aspects of these feminist utopias, such as a proper ecology, dearth of violence, increased tolerance, higher status for all types of work, female bonding, and alternative family and child-care structures.[3]
Dealing with such material demands new structures of narration, since as Nancy Hartsock suggests, "our conception of the world is itself a political choice."[4] In fiction, narrative technique regulates our conception. In science fiction which, by Darko Suvin's definition, involves estrangement from familiar standards and institutions, conception is all the more dependent on the mode of "telling." Marge Piercy comments on the crucial nature of form in her poem "A Shadow Play for Guilt."

    A man can lie to himself
    A man can lie with his tongue
    and his brain and his gesture;

> a man can lie with his life.
> But the body is simple as a turtle
> and straight as a dog:
> the body cannot lie.[5]

If Piercy believes her own message, surely her utopian Woman on the Edge of Time should offer an insight into the body, or form, or structure of feminist science fiction. In fact, because the novel describes both present-day New York City and a future Mattapoisett, it offers a comparison between traditional and utopian language use. I am concerned with how, by comparison of the techniques of narration used in the present and future worlds of Woman on the Edge of Time, Piercy and her characters discard what Russ calls the "old myths," and how, in fact, the novel demands that the reader look carefully at the injustices of these old myths in science fiction and in our culture.

Piercy's protagonist, Consuela Ramos, serves as a vehicle for an examination of the failings of our current language use. Since she is chicana, on welfare, and institutionalized for "lack of control and frustration tolerance" (though we learn the true nature of her behavior during the course of the novel), the chasm between her own life and that of members of the dominant white patriarchy is easily recognizable.[6] Language is one of the sociological markers of this chasm, and is used by members of that power structure as a tool of obfuscation rather than clarification. Technological diction, often a mainstay of extrapolative science fiction, is intended to exclude Connie from linguistic competence. That terms such as "microminiaturized" and "computer" might suggest significations within the ken of Connie and the other patients is never considered by the doctors who control their lives.

Assuming linguistic incompetence, the staff adopts a third person narrative stance regarding the patients, even in their presence. "We should get through this batch by two," (p. 91) Dr. Redding exclaims as Connie sits across the table from him. Both the use of the "royal we" and Redding's linguistic suggestion that patients are things rather than individuals exacerbate the social boundaries which already exist between them. Connie's isolation is also highlighted by speech acts regarding economics. While she drinks the water used to rinse out her coffee cup to "play her stomach an old trick," (p. 34) the doctors discuss medical care in terms of cost-efficiency and "foundation johnies."

The impersonal nature of this diction is echoed by Dolly, Connie's niece, who believes that the money she earns from prostitution will allow her to escape into the white middle class when she discusses her "johns." Piercy suggests that the jargon we take for granted as a commonality of American culture is not only impersonal, but also functions as a tool of classism. Language and class are most directly related in Louis, Connie's brother. As he begins to acquire the capital necessary to enter the dominant culture, he changes the pronunciation of his name from the Latin Luis to the Anglicized Lewis. For him, language is a path to social acceptance, similar to marriage; and he remarries three times, each successive wife more white than the last. Symbols of class consciousness remain impersonal.

Connie's class identification is easily seen through her use of Mexican-American slang. Ironically, most readers of Woman on the Edge of Time experience a fleeting moment of exclusion because this language isolates them from the protagonist's environment. However, Connie tends to break into native diction during moments unfamilar to middle-class readers. She uses Spanish when fighting with her niece's pimp, for instance; and the association of ethnic language with such events makes it clear which class the reader is being excluded from. While Connie compensates for her language by providing English equivalents for those she assumes have power over her, the doctors and social workers rarely make such linguistic concessions.

Umberto Eco argues that a word cannot become a sign unless members of the linguistic culture recognize and use it to identify some function repetitively.[7] Clearly, Connie's New York includes a sociology of language wherein members of the elite class can adjust signification according to their own desires. The denotative value of words is not absolute. When the hospital staff at Rockover State notices that Connie's hair is messy, they include a note in her dossier that she shows little concern for personal care. This system of meanings is then generalized to the entire language culture. Unfortunately, the signifier "messy hair" denotes something entirely different to those outside the power structure; there are no combs available in Connie's ward. This arbitrariness of signs creates a Kafkaesque sense for Connie and the other mental patients since they must continually try to decipher what their words and gestures mean to the members of the medical staff. Since Piercy presents this powerlessness from Connie's point of view, the reader begins to recognize how systems for reading signs, and the accepted value of words, must be called into question. At this point, Woman on the Edge of Time begins to challenge the language patterns of the dominant culture.

Mattapoisett, Piercy's future world of 2137, practices egalitarian linguistics. Connie learns of these new practices because of her capabilities as a "catcher." Luciente, a resident of Mattapoisett, has been experimenting with time travel; and it is Connie who becomes the initial contact. At first, communication proves difficult, primarily because of the many neologisms each must face while speaking "English" to one another. Connie's response is defensive: "Just because I'm Chicana and on welfare, don't try to tell me what poor vocabulary I speak with." (p. 42).

As their relationship develops, both Connie and her host begin to recognize that vocabulary is not the source of communication problems, but rather that, since Mattapoisett lacks a social hierarchy, the signifieds themselves are vastly different. Piercy, in her recent article "Mirror Images," states that the role of poetry (and in this case utopia fiction) is to affix names to familiar experiences which have not previously been identified.[8] Luciente's culture has done much of this work, in the process of evolving toward a utopian state. Particularly, rather than the economic and technological jargon of New York, they have created a language of social relation. If necessity is the mother of linguistic invention, as suggested by the lexical variety within Eskimo languages for words dealing with what English inaccurately calls snow, then a feminist utopia needs a language describing the complexity of social interaction. As Luciente informs Connie, "To explain anything exotic, you have to convey at once the thing and the vocabulary with which to talk about the thing . . . Your vocabulary is remarkably weak in words for mental states, mental abilities, and mental acts." (p. 42). Mattapoisett has created an effective vocabulary of human relation, as Connie learns in the following dialog with Luciente.

> "We're sweet friends. Some of us use the term 'core' for those we're closest to . . ."
> "Another lover!"
> "No, Otter's a hand friend, not a pillow friend. We've been close since we were sixteen. Politically we are very close." (p. 72).

Thus lexical improvement is essential to change. Additionally, new language undermines the stereotyping which hampers Connie, who, as a "chicana" and "mental patient" and "child-beater" must act according to certain social mores. She measures herself against these cultural standards constantly to the point where even her dreams meet the expectations of the dominant society; she would like two children and to "keep them clean as advertisements." (p. 47). It is these cultural standards, and the connotations associated with them, however, that guarantee that Connie will never become a member of mainstream society since the codes she must subscribe to demand embarrassing humility, underachievement, and a series of roles associated with age, race, sex, and class which preclude escape.

Walter Meyer, in <u>Aliens and Linguists</u>, states that science fiction neologism may maintain the denotative value of a familiar sign, while removing connotations.[9] This procedure is similar to that necessary for the elevation of stereotypes. Residents of Mattapoisett recognize this need and allow an escape from assigned meanings, beginning with individual naming. At adolescence, children are placed in natural isolation for a week or so. During this time, they must choose a new name for themselves; and it is by this moniker that they are known when they return to the village. They are allowed, in addition, to take on a new name whenever they change (or, in linguistic terms, whenever a new signified develops) with the caveat that "if you do it too often nobody remembers your name." (p. 77). Hence, the denotative value of a sign has been fixed at the level of naming; and this leads, presumably, to much greater accuracy of language use throughout the culture. For instance, even the meaning inherent in cats' gestures has been interpreted by 2137. Residents of the future are proud of their progress in communication; one of their eighteen major holidays is "Washoe Day," which commemorates the first animal (a monkey) to learn signs from another species (humans). This represents quite a change from Connie's environment where she finds it impossible to communicate essential information, such as the knowledge that her ribs have been broken, to members of her own species.

Piercy details the social institutions Mattapoisett employs to maintain their evolutionary language. Apparently, they are based on a social science much more sophisticated than our present efforts. They have discovered, by unidentified means, that "all the arts fall out in a forty/ sixty ratio in the population." (p. 75). Dialog also has become part of the fabric of society. After any argument, "the winners have to feed the loosers and give them presents." (pp. 153-4). The result is a set of social codes which guarantee continued dialog. If no other method succeeds, conflicting parties face institutionalized consciousness raising sessions called "worming." The purpose of this roundtable is to "comprehend that hostility and see if we can diffuse it." (p. 207). While such transactive methods may seem hopelessly optimistic to Connie, the lesson she learns from them is not. When Luciente teaches Connie to appear unconscious, as a step toward escape from the mental institution, only her power of hearing remains. Connie, and through her, the reader, finds in Mattapoisett a culture which realizes that maintaining structures of communication is essential to change.

Piercy points out that, in order to change, language must be recognized as a synchronically changing entity. Mainstream literary criticism has battled with the problem that language never produces an absolute set of significances. Current critics such as Bloom and Derrida, in particular, recognize how history forces constant reinterpretation of cultural data, of which language is the common denominator. Perhaps, no art form has shown us this more clearly than science fiction in its American evolution since the time of Gernsback's Amazing. The predictions of those early future visions have passed, as Robert Scholes notes; and the future has now become history. If nothing else, science fiction has taught us to see past, present, and future as part of a continuum.[10]

Luciente recognizes the evolutionary nature of language, and after telling a story in which Harriet Tubman is confused with Sojourner Truth, and the slaves sack the Pentagon, she admits that "history gets telescoped a little." (p. 173). Language here has no pretense to absolute value, after all. Consequently, neither does art, history, nor politics. Recognizing this, Connie learns of her own political value for the first time. As Barbarossa explains, "at certain cruxes of history . . . forces are in conflict. Technology is imbalanced. Too few have too much power. Alternative futures are equally or almost equally probable . . . and that affects the . . . shape of time." (p. 197). This is Connie's greatest single revelation throughout the course of Woman on the Edge of Time. Interestingly, immediately before she begins this journey to selfunderstanding, Connie finds a pen that works. Like Luciente's language, Connie's pen is capable of accurately recording thought. Both are tools of change.

To this point, I have attempted a comparative analysis of the sociology of language in the two major cultures of Woman on the Edge of Time. I would now like to take one step further back, to examine how Piercy employs narrative techniques and inverts science fiction formula to attack the readers, in their relatively protected position as disinterested voyeurs, and demand that they become active participants in the text. I first suspected such manipulation of narration might be in evidence because of the angry reactions the New York portions of the novel evoked from many of my students who claimed, to paraphrase roughly, that they felt Piercy was "knocking them over the heads" with ghetto description. From a generic perspective, this evaluation may be accurate. For a science fiction novel, and even a critical utopia, Piercy includes more here-and-now description than is common to the time travel formula.

In the terms of science fiction criticism, however, Piercy also strives to "estrange" or "defamiliarize" the reader during the New York portions of her novel. Perception becomes automatic as it becomes habitual, says Victor Shklovshy, and therefore the purpose of art is to make the world unfamiliar, thereby "prolonging perception."[11] Mattapoisett, like most science fiction settings, is already estranged in time and place, but by means of Piercy's narrative technique, present-day New York also becomes estranged; the present functions as science fiction.

This begins with an inversion of one of the commonplaces of science fiction definition; Russ calls it "What If Literature."[12] Michael Holquist goes on to suggest that utopias in particular produce a "what if time," and that, therefore, they "are the literature of the subjunctive mood."[13] Yet, the subjunctive, because of its formal nature and its usual association with hypothetical and nonfactual statements, separates reader and text. This separation is heightened in utopian fiction where gaps of time and place occur. Hence, both grammatically and cosmologically, utopia tends to be the most fictional of science fiction forms. It is this fictional distance which may lull the reader into a comfortable sense of safety. Piercy counteracts fictional distance by placing the tense of utopia, subjunctive mood, in the present. Because of Connie's own distance from the dominant patriarchy, she is faced with "what if" in her own environment, rather than in the future world she discovers. Connie owns a pragmatics based on possibility. "When blocked, maneuver to survive. The first rule of life inside." (p. 24). If I had street clothes, then I could escape. If I steal parathion, then I could poison the doctors who wish to alter my brain. If I fight back now, perhaps my children's children's children will grow up in Luciente's utopia. In Woman on the Edge of Time, the subjunctive is the literature of the here and now.

Piercy emphasizes the crucial nature of the present and demands the reader do so also by modulating narrative complexity. Most of the events in the two future visions are narrated in what Genette calls "scene" where, in the fashion of the realistic novel, the time of narration of event appears equal to the time of the event. A great majority of these passages involve lengthy dialog in present tense, again a relatively natural means of telling a story. However, Connie inhabits a much more complex narrative world in New York. While her story, moving from Dolly's entrance to the trip back to Rockover State, progresses through a series of scenes, this linear narration is interrupted by summaries and ellipses.

Connie also is given to what Genette calls "external analepses," which occur when she flashes back to moments such as her Mexican childhood which occurred before the beginning of the central story in the novel. Additionally, her mandated use of thorazine prevents lucid thinking so she often repeats memories, always ignoring certain data that would make these memories completed narrative units. Montage, familiar to twentieth century readers but emphasized here because of its juxtaposition with the simpler Mattapoisett narrative, results. The sense is one of discovering Connie's history, particularly the parts of it defined by men (her lovers, past employer, and Claud and Martin). The present and its power structure is emphasized by the relatively more complex narration, demanding that the reader scrutinize what appears.

A dialectical tension intrinsic to New York escalates this emphasis. This tension is missing in Mattapoisett. Holquist notes that this is also characteristic of utopian fictions. "Society ceases to be a live organism in the utopia. It becomes rather a machine for manufacturing that type of man [sic] which the author sees as the best man."[14] Though he here overlooks the type of utopia which has institutionalized an aesthetic of change, such as Woman on the Edge of Time or Charnas' Motherlines, his sentiment that utopias try to expunge conflicting values is valid. Mattapoisett finds its antithesis in Gildena's New York, which appears in an alternative time continuum. In that future, class structure is exaggerated. Yet, as Joanna Russ menacingly observes, "if the utopias stress a feeling of harmony and connection with the natural world, the authors may be telling us that in reality they feel a lack of such connection."[15] This understates the case in Woman on the Edge of Time where Piercy's present vision captures the huge hiatus between these in and out of power. Utopias may remove conflicts intrinsic to their cultures, as Piercy shows. However, by placing the source of the conflicts between alternative futures in the present world, Connie becomes the focus of the science fiction novel. She is, after all, the one who must untangle the various strands of the continua of time.

Piercy continues to elevate the New York portions of her novel to science fiction, or, more accurately, dystopia, by the use of the fantastic. According to Eric Rabkin, the fantastic occurs whenever groundrules established by a text are contradicted within that text. A change of genre, style, implied author, logical sequence, character, or any other element of fiction may be responsible for the fantastic, which "does more than extend experience; [it] contradicts perspectives."[16] Rabkin's definition reads like a literary version of an anarchist politic. I would argue that this is exactly what Piercy is after in Woman on the Edge of Time, and that her narration of Connie's life constantly contradicts the groundrules of science fiction. The political intent of such narration is identified by Rabkin when he says "by understanding the mental reversals implicit in a realistic novel [which includes elements of the fantastic], we can see the dialectic relations possible between external and internal groundrules."[17] In other words, the fantastic forces a reader to become more self-conscious.

Even the total shape of the novel contradicts genre expectations for the adventure formula though Connie tries

to maintain them. She tries to picture events in an
Aristotelean sense, replete with beginning, middle, and
end. As a socialized member of contemporary society, she
expects certain patterns and rhythms of existence. She
tries to complete her "pattern," which makes up the New
York part of Woman on the Edge of Time, by poisoning her
doctors, a conclusion fit for any adventure story. However,
her contacts with Luciente contradict the groundrule of
closure. Luciente does not tell stories which "end." When
Connie tries to fashion a climactic battle scene to "conclude"
the war around Mattapoisett, Piercy quickly points out that
such an ending was only hallucination. Like Connie, our
perceptions of closure are contradicted by Mattapoisett,
producing the fantastic. But the world itself does not
always develop in linear fashion, Piercy seems to be saying,
even though TV sitcoms and naturalistic novels often depict
life in those terms. Children in Mattapoisett are taught
this leasson early, through a game called "Web," which,
unlike our goal oriented hide-and-seek, allows each player
a strand which is woven amongst those of the other children.
Luciente herself sides with those who take a non-linear view
of bioengineering; she is a "mixer," favoring a random gene
pool, rather than a "shaper," one who would like planned
eugenics.

Piercy contradicts many of our cultural perceptions as
well. Foremost among these are the sex roles endorsed by
current society. Connie carries these socialized values
with her, and exploits them as a way to get what she needs
from the hospital staff. Unfortunately, Luciente does not
conform to Connie's ready-made sexual categories, even though
the latter tries to place the former in nearly all of them:
Male on the make, gay male, butch, femme, and finally,
friend. Partially, this confusion results because the
residents of Mattapoisett often combine the biological
features of both sexes. This process of combining sexual
markers is negated in Gildena's future where sex roles are
excruciatingly clearly defined. However, other pop culture
artifacts are recombined. Gildena mentions the "richies,"
who include the "Rockemellons, the Morganfords, the Duke-Ponts."
(p. 297). These lucky few control production through a
monopoly named "Chase-World-TT." (p. 300). More than
humorous game-playing, the process of recombining familiar
artifacts challenges the myths built around them and begins
a process of social commentary.[18]

A final category of the fantastic includes Piercy's use of
science fiction conventions. While these groundrules are
contradicted at various points throughout Woman on the Edge
of Time, perhaps one example central to Connie's development
might be mentioned. This is the trope of the "first contact"
ambassador. Luciente, the visitor to our culture, remains a
perfect model of the disinterested spectator. Though many
aspects of our environment offend her, such as the internal
combustion engine and the dearth of leisure time, she is
aware that no interference is allowed. Connie, however,
who assumes the role of ambassador based on her psi powers,
frequently tries to alter what she doesn't like. Her
indignation at new mores appears often, as when she sees
two children experimenting with sex, unsuccessfully.

I have tried to show how Piercy's manipulation of narration emphasizes the faults of our present culture, and particularly our language, in Woman on the Edge of Time. Mattapoisett provides a solution to these issues, and that use of subjunctive mood, narrative complexity, and the fantastic effectively turn the "realistic" portion of the novel into science fiction as a means toward this emphasis. The novel includes one final technique to identify the power structures which cripple characters: exaggeration. Gildena's New York, on an alternative continuum ostensibly brought into focus by Connie's failure to fight back against her doctors, contains all the worst aspects of language failure and stratification. Gildena's language is filled with euphemism; "dead," an illegal word, has become "ashed." Deceptive codes and acronyms conceal oppressive social practices; every one is "SG'd" (segregated and guarded), and all women must be "opped" (cosmetic surgery to make them attractive for men). Jargon prevents language from communicating across the linguistic community. Most importantly, the language of this distasteful future confirms the position of women as property, since each is a "contracty," which can include anything from "lesby sex" to birthing. New York, our world, occurs at a crux in time. The polarities between Luciente and Gildena are included, as yet unsorted, in Connie.

Changing behavior is difficult. But, as Luciente's "core" friend tells Connie, "we have found no way to break dependencies without some risk. What we can't risk is our people remaining stuck in old patterns." (p. 116). By comparing contemporary New York culture with a utopian future, Piercy has created a science fiction narrative which "defamiliarizes" the reader along with the protagonist, challenging both to adopt a radical mode of thinking. It is a utopian novel which forces us to look at ourselves. This type of thinking, characterized by William Appleman Williams as the "ruthless analysis" necessary to radical perspectives, is essential to Piercy's novel, and her view of the women's movement.[19] If feminism hopes to continue to use science fiction as a tool aimed at entertainment and enlightenment, then we must understand the implications of structures of narration. Woman on the Edge of Time examines the effects of just a few of these structures, and just a few of the possible solutions.

The University of Colorado

Notes

[1] Joanna Russ. "What Can a Heroine Do? or Why Women Can't Write," in Images of Women in Fiction, ed. Susan Koppelman Cornillon (Bowling Green: Bowling Green University Press, 1972).

[2] Robert Jewett and John Shelton Lawrence, The American Monomyth.

[3] See Carol Pearson's "Coming Home: Four Feminist Utopias and Patriarchal Experience" and Joanna Russ' "Recent Feminist

Utopias." Both appear in Future Females: A Critical Anthology, ed. Marlene [sic] Barr (Bowling Green: Bowling Green State University Popular Pess, 1981).

[4]Nancy Hartsock, "Feminist Theory and the Development of Revolutionary Strategy," in Capitalist Patriarchy and the Case for Socialist Feminism, ed. Zillah R. Eisenstein (New York: Monthly Review Press, 1979), p. 56.

[5]Marge Piercy, Circles on the Water (New York: Alfred Knopf, 1982), p. 84.

[6]Marge Piercy, Woman on the Edge of Time (New York: Fawcett Crest, 1976), p. 91. All future references will be to this edition.

[7]Umberto Eco, A Theory of Semiotics (Bloomington: Indiana University Press, 1976), p. 24.

[8]Marge Piercy, "Mirror Images," in Women's Culture, ed. Gayle Kimball (Metuchen, NJ: Scarecrow Press, 1981), p. 188.

[9]Walter Meyers, Aliens and Linguists (Athens, GA: University of Georgia Press, 1980), p. 8.

[10]Robert Scholes, Structural Fabulation, p. 13.

[11]Daphne Patai, "When Women Rule: Defamiliarization in the Sex-Role Reversal Utopia," in Extrapolation, 23:1 (1982), 57.

[12]Joanna Russ, "Images of Women in Science Fiction," in Cornillon, 79.

[13]Michael Holquist, "How to Play Utopia: Some Brief Notes on the Distinctiveness of Utopian Fiction," in Science Fiction, ed. Mark Rose (Englewood Cliffs, NJ: Prentice Hall, 1976), p. 139.

[14]Holquist, p. 140.

[15]Russ, "Recent Feminist Utopias," p. 81.

[16]Eric Rabkin, The Fantastic in Literature (Princeton: Princeton University Press, 1976), p. 4.

[17]Rabkin, p. 216.

[18]Russ, "What Can a Heroine Do? or Why Women Can't Write," pp. 6-7.

[19]William Appleman Williams, "Radicals and Regionalism," in Democracy, 1:4 (Oct. 1981), p. 88.

Marleen Barr

The Metalinguistic Racial Grammar of Bellona:
Ethnicity, Language and Meaning in Samuel R. Delany's
Dhalgren

Dhalgren is difficult to read and at times seems to be incomprehensible. The nature of its language, not plot or characterization details, is the most compelling aspect of the novel, a work which begins and ends with incomplete sentences. My essay first offers a brief theoretical explanation of the function of metalinguistics in both Dhalgren and the science fiction genre. This introduction is followed by a practical discussion of how Delany's idiosyncratic (or metalinguistic) style, his definitions of which are uniquely pertinent to the novel's text, illustrates the reality of racism in contemporary America.

* * *

In addition to positing new worlds and cultures, science fiction presents new possibilities for language. For example, Delany explains that the following sentence's meaning would differ in science fiction and mundane texts: "She gave her heart willingly."[1] We would not expect the heroine of a Harlequin romance to voluntarily open her chest cavity, wrench her heart from within, and present it to her beloved on a silver platter. This might be perfectly acceptable behavior for a science fiction heroine, however. In addition to Delany, critics Eric S. Rabkin and Larry McCaffery also remind us that readers must learn a slightly different code in order correctly to interpret science fiction texts. The genre's readers must be open to the idea that familiar words can be given new meanings. McCaffery comments upon these fresh insights:

> If literature is viewed as a game, governed primarily by internal rules of consistency rather than by allegiance to outer laws or conditions, it becomes quite natural for

writers to wish to explore literary games which can be played with fresher, more vital rules . . . new patterns of perception were developed. . . . new games with new rules and new meanings can always be imagined. . . . the potential always exists for new combinations, new insights, new fictional patterns which can free us from exhausted perceptual systems.[2]

Dhalgren includes such liberating--and playful--new linguistic rules, meanings, and combinations of old material. The presentation of its different fantastic world is dependent upon the presentation of its different use of language. For example, as I will later explain in greater detail, within the world of Dhalgren, the word "nigger" applies to every character regardless of race or economic position. The novel's special use of this word coincides with Rabkin's notions about metalinguistics and science fiction: "'. . . the text can use language as the material it cuts and patterns and sews into new creations not necessarily having anything to do overtly with the linguistic materials. . . . [science fiction] authors have taken linguistic material with which we are familiar and transformed it."[3] Dhalgren contains many examples of "the particular metalinguistic function of treating the reader's language as material for transformation." (R. p. 87). It moves toward granting the wish of the protagonist of Donald Barthelme's Snow White: "'Oh I wish there were some words in the world that were not the words I always hear.'" (M. p. 30). The number of words in a science fiction text that can be changed must of course be limited. (Even the changes Anthony Burgess made to develop the apparently new language in his A Clockwork Orange could not all be unconventional.) McCaffery explains that because they cannot completely discard old conventions, generating new forms becomes a problem for contemporary writers: "The artistic issue is central to contemporary fiction: how to escape from stale conventions . . . while yet not acknowledging that certain fundamental patterns remain essential to the artists in defining our existence. . . . [There is a] conflict between the desire to seek the new completely outside prior patterns and the belief that the new can only be defined in terms of the past . . ." (M. p. 30). Dhalgren grapples with this problem by giving some familiar words and word patterns new definitions. This creative act can be explained by paraphrasing Snow White's wish: within the text of Dhalgren, there are some definitions in the world that are not the definitions she always hears. These new definitions are "not quite our own language, though like enough to it that we can map the transformations and know their causes." (R. p. 86).

Linguistic transformations make a reality claim for a science fiction text: ". . . transformed language . . . makes a reality claim for the fantastic world, arguing implicitly for its potential dire truth. . . . all metalinguistic uses of language . . . [assert] a linguistic connectedness between writer and reader and hence implicitly . . . [claim] a sort of reality for the fictional world." (R. pp. 87, 89). The causes of the language transformations in Dhalgren both make a reality claim for the novel and stem from Delany's experiences as a black person living in a racist society. Hence, the reality that metalinguistics claims for Dhalgren's fantastic world is not limited to its text. Delany's new definitions also enable him to make statements about the dire truth of racism in the real world he shares with the reader.

Dhalgren, then, takes full advantage of science fiction's metalinguistic characteristics. This essay will now go on to present a detailed discussion of the novel's insistence upon specific interpretations which are limited to its own textual world. It will also show that, in addition to making a reality claim for the fantastic world within the novel, the text's metalinguistic aspects relate to the real world.

* * *

Only readers of Dhalgren would use the famous appellation "George Harrison" when referring to a newly discovered second moon which bears a black man's name. Portrayals of ethnicity in Dhalgren resemble this peculiar designation: they are discussed in terms which readers must learn to interpret. And as the text announces, like the language of the novel, the language of Bellona, Dhalgren's ruined city, is not universally understood: "We speak another language here. . . . Is there any line in it, [a pamphlet] however, that would be comprehensible outside city limits?"[4] Many of the novel's most important references to ethnicity would not be comprehensible outside its pages and are not mentioned directly.

This statement applies to George Harrison, a dark moon visible only as a white reflection, a black man's name universally recognized as belonging to a white musician. Similarly, American culture which is derived from black experience--dance, music, and fashion for example--is usually seen only in terms of white culture. Further, the novel's huge sun, its second metaphysical heavenly body, emphasizes that true blackness remains when the source of white reflections is removed? "'When it [the oversized sun] goes all the way down, there won't be any fuckin' light at all, again . . . ever' . . . 'Black as a fucking bitch . . . yeah!'" (p. 492). Like this enlarged sun, white cultural hegemony,--the power to falsely reflect black culture--is unnaturally oversized.

The recognition given to George Harrison is part of the fantastic. Americans have always named extraterrestrial bodies after white people. Harrison also exemplifies black people's real experience. In Bellona and in America, only Caucasians like Kamp--the novel's astronaut--not blacks like George, have traveled to the moon. Kamp discusses his moon exploration in terms of color and meaning and suggests that Bellona's two moons symbolize the presence of America's black and white cultures:

> ' . . . it's [the moon] another world, and when you're there, you have no way of knowing what anything means. Physically. The moon is a different world, with a different order that you don't understand. There isn't that richness--not because it isn't in bright colors, or because it's all brown, purple and grey. It's because

as you run your eyes over the rocks and dirt, you have no
way to know what the tiny alterations in color mean.
(p. 678).

Black neighborhoods such as Bellona's Jackson are another
world to white people. They have difficulty discerning
meaning when venturing into the black world. On the other
hand, in the white world, color differences result in the
eradication, what Tillie Olsen would call the "silencing,"
of those differences.[5] So far, for example, black people's
access to space exploration has been silenced or eradicated.
Black citizens' experience of the moon is a reflection of
white men's experience.

Like George Harrison, Madame Brown also contributes to
the racial grammar of Bellona. She is the most normal and
most professional person in the novel, a social worker who
is friend and sometimes protector to the white Richards
family. Despite her name, this reader immediately assumed
that Mrs. Brown was white. Delany leads readers, at least
white readers, to automatically generate this assumption.
(Cultural hegemony is an element of readers' responses.)
His text does not provide correct information until page 844:
"'Do they even know you're black? . . . Do they [the Richards]
know you're gay?' 'Let me see,' she said after a moment:
'Black, lesbian, I'm also very middle class.'" (pp. 844-45).
Unlike sexual preference, race is--of course--easily discerned. Delany is acting purposefully playful. The sarcastic
suggestion that the Richards can fail to recognize Mrs.
Brown's blackness points to the aforementioned pervasive
silencing of black culture. There is more sarcasm: when
readers are first introduced to a character named Muriel,
there is no indication that instead of being a Jewish woman,
Muriel is Mrs. Brown's dog.

In Delany's portrayals of Mrs. Brown and Muriel, black
fuses with white, woman fuses with dog. Two characters'
following comments evoke another ethnic merger: "'I'm
black. You're white. You can't have a black soul.' . . .
'Most of the time you come on pretty white to me.'" (p. 327).
Their conversation is quite pointless within the world of the
novel. Regardless of the literal color of their skin, everyone in Bellona experiences ethnic merger; everyone is a
"nigger." Because of Bellona's technological breakdown, all
citizens live in substandard housing, all must make survival
their first priority. As they proceed through Bellona's
smoky environment under the two moons and the enlarged sun,
everyone in Bellona is "black." All of Bellona is Jackson.

Cities, as the text tells us, are capable of generating
meanings and myths about their inhabitants: "Because that
means it's the city. That means its the landscape and the
bricks, and the girders, and the faulty wiring and the shot
elevator machinery, all conspiring together to make these
myths true." (p. 278). Because Bellona's urban decay is
experienced equally by blacks and white, because everyone in
the city is a nigger, the myths and meanings--and realities--
usually reserved for poor American blacks are part of the
lives of people like the Richards. They live in a burned
out building; Mr. Richards is financially and emotionally
ineffective; his wife suffers while trying to hold the family

together; their son's death directly results from their
dwelling's physical decay. In addition, the Richards are
niggers because of the special meaning the novel's world
attributes to their street. The text explains:

> 'What kind of street do they live on?' In the grammar
> of another city, that sentence would hold the implication:
> What kind of street are they more or less constrained
> by society to live on, given their semioutlaw status
> . . . and the economics of their asocial position. In
> Bellona, however, the same words imply a complex freedom,
> a choice from hovel to mansion--complex because every
> hovel and every mansion sustains through that choice some
> remnant of our ineffable catastrophe. (p. 830).

Bellona's complex freedom: the breakdown of technology
causes the breakdown of differentiations between the lives
of blacks and whites. In the racial grammar of Bellona,
privation usually endured by blacks becomes part of white
experiential vocabulary.

Stereotypical white and black experiences merge because
of the fantastic nature of Bellona. Further, the text, in
accordance with Delany's notion that science fiction is in
dialogue with the real present and that there is a relationship between world and word, points to the truth of racial
separatism. For example, the sentence "Multiple Caucasian
laughter fell down through the spiral railing." (p. 529).
Even an arch bigot would not argue for the superiority of
Caucasian laughter. Sometimes the text's references to
racism are less subtle: "'It was a white boy, too' . . .
'And he gonna come all the way down here to shoot niggers.'"
(p. 521).

There is nothing metalinguistic about these sentences, no
special meaning pertinent only to the grammar of Bellona.
Yet, because of Bellona's fantastic technologically flawed
environment, racism in Bellona is somehow more ludicrous than
racism in the real world. The differences between Fifth
Avenue and Harlem might explain the presence of racist
myths. These myths persist in Bellona even though the city's
environment is uniformly wretched.

In other words, the presence and implications of racism
in Bellona are absurd. More specifically, in the pages
(719-21) preceding the point where readers learn that their
perception of the novel's structure and the protagonist's
endeavors are false, they are informed that blacks have
set fire to their section of the city. George Harrison
describes the fire in terms of moon and sun imagery:

> 'Niggers done set the whole of Jackson to burning, don't
> it look like?' ' . . . Look at that burn, burn up like
> a motherfucker; it's beautiful, huh? Like walking in the
> sun' . . . 'The moon get its light from the sun and shine
> all night' . . . 'It burn and it burn and it never stop.
> It send the folk all down running through the city of the
> sun. . . .' (p. 719).

Why should a uniformly substandard city have a separate black
area? Why should a "race riot" occur in a city where blacks

and whites experience equal privation?

The answers become apparent as the protagonist comments on Dhalgren's text: "But as one reads along, one becomes more and more suspicious that the author has lost the thread of his argument, that the questions will never be resolved, or more upsetting, that the position of the characters will have so changed by the book's end that the answers to the initial questions will have become trivial. (It is Troy, Sodom, Abel Cuyuk, the city of Dreadful . . ." (p. 322). This is true of the language of racism: emotions skew the logic of arguments and questions are never resolved. When members of one ethnic group improve their economic position, logical answers to questions regarding racism become trivial.

Bellona is every American city. Regardless of all circumstances, regardless of how equal the lives of blacks and whites become, racism and separatism will still exist. There is no completely effective escape from racism; its presence is ever on going, circular, like the moon and the sun, like the circular metalinguistic structure of Dhalgren.

Virginia Technological and State University

Notes

[1] All direct references to Delany are derived from the keynote address he delivered at the International Conference on the Fantastic in the Arts, March 1982.

[2] Larry McCaffery, "Form, Formula, and Fantasy: Generative Structures in Contemporary Fiction," in George E. Slusser, Eric S. Rabkin, and Robert Scholes, Bridges to Fantasy (Carbondale and Edwardsville: Southern Illinois University Press, 1982), pp. 27, 35, 36. Further references to this article will appear in the text followed by M and page number.

[3] Eric S. Rabkin, "Metalinguistics and Science Fiction," Critical Inquiry, 6 (Autumn 1979), 81, 86. Further references to this article will appear in the text followed by R and page number.

[4] Samuel R. Delany, Dhalgren (New York: Bantam Books, 1975), p. 830. Further references will appear in the text followed by the appropriate page number.

[5] See Tillie Olsen, Silences (New York: Delacorte/Seymour Lawrence, 1978).

Joseph F. Patrouch, Jr.

Harlan Ellison's Use of the Narrator's Voice

    Let's start with Chaucer. When Chaucer was writing
Troilus and Criseyde and The Canterbury Tales, literacy was
still confined to a fortunate few. The great majority of
people entertained by stories did not read them; they heard
them read. Still extant is a manuscript illumination showing
Chaucer reading aloud. In the background is a many-parapeted
castle perched on a wooded hill. In the center Chaucer
stands in a raised, vine-covered outdoor pulpit. And in
the foreground various colorfully clad men and women sit,
kneel, and stand. Most seem to be attending to the reading.
One fellow in particular, in the lower right, stands with
his elbows in the fork of a tree, his chin supported by his
right fist, his gaze fixed on Chaucer. At his feet, however,
sit a man and a woman staring rapturously into one another's
eyes, clearly paying no attention to Chaucer or anyone else.
Apparently no audience gives its full attention to any
reader.
    Perhaps Chaucer is reading from Troilus and Criseyde. In
this rather lengthy poem Chaucer pretends to be translating
an old poem out of "Lollius" for the edification of his
listeners. He appears in this poem, not as a participant
in the action (which is set in the besieged city of Troy),
but as a speaking voice commenting upon the people and
events he is modernizing. Perhaps he is reading The House
of Fame, in which he recounts how in a dream he is snatched
from a desert by a querulous eagle and carried away to an
allegorical palace in the sky. Or perhaps he is reading
"The Wife of Bath's Tale," in which case the audience would
be listening to Chaucer pretending to be the Wife of Bath
pretending to be a Loathely Lady lecturing her handsome young
husband on their wedding night, and wondering if all Arthurian
knights behaved so coldly as he was behaving towards her!
Chaucer had a wide variety of reading voices. He could be
the author commenting on the story at hand, or an actual

character named Geoffrey, or some other persona, some other character he has created. Even when the author reads his works aloud (so that the speaking voice is clearly his) a variety of roles is still possible.

From Chaucer's time on into the nineteenth century the speaking voice of a story was meant to be listened to. People read aloud to one another for entertainment. Jane Austen wrote her novels with the intention only of reading them aloud to her friends and relatives, and not for publication. Printing and the gradual spread of literacy made the reading aloud of stories (and the listening to such performances) available to more and more people. What is considered today the flaw of the auctoral intrusion (the author interrupting his own story to speak in his own voice to the readers) was then a natural and expected part of reading aloud to a listening audience. The words were being spoken aloud by real people, what more natural than that the speaker should occasionally speak out directly to the people before him.

But something happened in the twentieth century. So many people became able to read for themselves that they no longer needed to be read to. The audience stopped being listeners to stories and became readers of stories. The speaking voice disappeared, and the nature of fiction changed radically. When one is sitting alone in a chair reading silently, why listen to oneself tell oneself a story, and why direct asides and editorial comments to oneself? As the author as speaking voice faded away, the author as arranger of human experience came to the fore.

The best definition of twentieth-century fiction that I can think of is "vicarious human experience." The book one is holding, the chair one is sitting in, the room that surrounds one all should fade away under the assault of those powerful little black marks on the white pages. One merges with the narrative point of view character in the story and sees only what that character sees (not the print on the page) and hears only what he hears (not a voice telling a story). Each of us lives his life inside his own head. It makes no difference whether the experiences that shape our personalities and our value systems get into our pasts and our behaviors from "real" life or from the printed page. "Really" or "vicariously" we have experienced it. And that is the mark of twentieth-century fiction, that it is vicarious human experience.

Because they were the kind of stories editors were looking for, Harlan Ellison broke into writing in the mid-fifties doing neat little formula stories for mystery magazines, SF magazines, men's magazines. Since then his writing has developed in any number of ways, the chief of which I have discussed elsewhere, in an essay called "Harlan Ellison and the Formula Story" (The Book of Ellison, ed. Andrew Porter [New York], 1978). There I chronicled in some detail his movement from the structured formula story to the more flexible form-is-determined-by-content kind of story he now writes, from the neat problem-solving of "Life Hutch" to the probing character development of "Croatoan." Here I want to look at the re-emergence of the speaking voice in Ellison's fiction.

When Ellison began his career in the fifties, he wrote stories to send to editors to publish for people who then read them alone and to themselves. The stories were for the reader's eyes and mind, not for the reader's ears. As a result the stories tend to be about one person who the reader becomes for the duration of the reading experience. The information the reader is given is information collected by and through this one character: what he hears, sees, thinks, what happens around him that he is aware of. "Life Hutch," Ellison's second published story (his first was the infamous "Glow Worm," too awful to take seriously) begins this way:

> Terrence slid his right hand, the one out of sight of the robot, up his side. The razoring pain of the three broken ribs caused his eyes to widen momentarily in pain. Then he recovered himself and closed them till he was studying the machine through narrow slits.
> If the eyeballs click, I'm dead, thought Terrence.

From the very first word the reader knows who he is supposed to be. From that word on, the reader is Terrence. The author stays behind the scenes, controlling the illusion but not intruding upon it. This is vicarious human experience, and there is no speaking voice.

In contrast, this is the opening of Ellison's Hugo-winning, 1973 story "The Deathbird":

> This is a test. Take notes. This will count as 3/4 of your final grade. Hints: remember, in chess, kings cancel each other out and cannot occupy adjacent squares, are therefore all-powerful and totally powerless, cannot affect one another, produce stalemate. Hinduism is a polytheistic religion; the sect of Atman worships the divine spark of life with Man; in effect saying, "Thou art God." Provisos of equal time are not served by one viewpoint having media access to two hundred million people in prime time while opposing viewpoints are provided with a soapbox on the corner. Not everyone tells the truth. Operational note: these sections may be taken out of numerical sequence: rearrange to suit yourself for the optimum clarity. Turn over your test papers and begin.

The contrast with a story like "Life Hutch" couldn't be greater. All the questions which one would normally ask of the kind of fiction which is vicarious human experience are simply irrelevant. The reader is not supposed to become any one else while he is reading this story. He remains himself, listening to Ellison.

Two more recent examples will perhaps help clarify the point. "Grail" and "Night of Black Glass" were both published in 1981 and now have been republished in Stalking the Nightmare. The question to ask is this: are we listening to Ellison tell us about the characters, or are we being asked to become the characters?

"Grail":
Years later, when he was well into young adulthood, Christopher Caperton wrote about it in the journal he had begun to keep when he turned twenty-one. The entry had everything to do with the incident, though he had totally forgotten it.

What he wrote was this: The great tragedy of my life is that in my search for the Holy Grail everyone calls True Love, I see myself as Zorro, a romantic and mysterious highwayman--and the women I desire see me as Porky Pig.

The incident lost to memory that informed his observation had taken place fourteen years earlier, in 1953, when he was thirteen years old.

"Night of Black Glass":
When he finally made the decision to slip off the end of the world, he took only one hundred dollars from the joint account, left Gwen no note, went to the Greyhound station and slipped fifty of the hundred through the window to the clerk, and said, "Send me as far as this will take me."

He wound up on the rocky coast of Maine.

He had never been to Maine, and he had no particular interest in going to Maine; but he wanted to walk off the end of the world and Maine was as likely a departure point as any. Was there still a Timbuktu?

Clearly we are not being asked to become either of these people. We are being asked to sit still and listen to Ellison tell us about them. Ellison has brought back, in his fiction, the speaking voice, a device used by Chaucer and Milton, and by the great nineteenth-century novelists, but abandoned in this century when reading became a private rather than a public pleasure. Surely this is because Ellison (as had Chaucer, Dickens, and Twain before him) reads his stories aloud to audiences. At an Ellison performance there is a voice in the air, an interlocutor (if you will) between the material and the audience. Just as it was silly for the individual reader to tell himself a story (which accounts for the disappearance of the speaking voice from fiction early in this century), so it would be silly for Ellison to pretend he had no audience at his readings and to write for that person sitting alone in a room reading silently to himself.
Ellison is telling us these marvelous stories, and he does it so well we sit and listen--in the large lecture hall when he is present on the stage to fill our ears and in the isolation of the small room when he is present on the page to fill our eyes. It is Harlan Ellison's voice and personality that has come to dominate his work.

University of Dayton

Thom Dunn

The Social Science Fiction of Robin Cook

To date Robin Cook has written four sensational formula thrillers including Coma (1977), a novel of organ transplantation and anesthesia, highly popular since its appearance in movie form, and three more recent and less well known novels: Sphinx (1979), of Egyptology and the theft of antiquities, Brain (1981), another novel of body snatching in a big city hospital, and Fever (1982), of cancer treatment and toxic wastes. All are fast-paced, indeed breathless, page-turners in which the hapless protagonist, an Ordinary Person but for her scientific knowledge and investigatory zeal, is propelled by the best motives of rescue and self-sacrifice through a sleeples Walpurgisnacht of horror thrust upon her by a community far gone in apathy and greed.

My interest in Cook came about through the simple urge to find a good read--I did--and the subsequent desire to uncover critical comment about his work--I did not. It is not surprising that Cook's work has not thusfar been gathered among the fruits of the MLA: his plots are outrageously contrived and his characters move like puppets and talk like people in a detergent commercial; but it is curious that no study, to my knowledge, of Cook has been undertaken by those of us pledged to examine popular literature in an academic context.[1] It is even stranger that Cook has been ignored by the makers of science fiction summas, even the best of which, Peter Nicholls' Science Fiction Encyclopedia, makes no mention whatever of him.[2]

Is all this as it should be? Is Cook not worth our attention? Should I put his books back on the "Thriller" shelf where they perhaps belong and write a paper instead on "The Use of the Definite Article in the Earthsea Trilogy?" Or does our ignorance of Cook bespeak a failing on our part to broaden the scope of our investigations to include science fiction regardless of how it is marketed?[3] At least in the case of Cook, I argue, our neglect is blamewrothy. We should

include Cook in our studies, not because his hack fiction is
no worse than others' but because his books are fact-and
process-oriented, exploring the facts and processes of
science, technology, industry, and the administrative systems
behind them all.[4] Moreover, in a tradition venerable in
social science fiction, Cook launches a strident attack
against bureaucratic bungling, malevolence, and sloth which
is a match in its relentless ferocity for Ken Kesey's One
Flew Over the Cuckoo's Nest or Marge Piercy's Woman on the
Edge of Time. Cook does for his topics what these writers
do for care of the mentally ill.

His critique follows this pattern: A scientist-protagonist
in the pursuit of her specialty (two are women, two men)
stumbles upon corruption at the very center of her world.
Being fundamentally decent, she cannot ignore the evil discovered, but when she attempts to inform the Powers she is
denounced, cast out, and threatened with death. Except for
Sphinx, an epilogue points the moral of each story, and in
Coma and Brain this takes the form of an Author's Note de-
tailing, with documentation, real-world examples of the
techno-horror thus combated.

In Coma, medical student Susan Wheeler discovers that O. R.
patients are being purposely rendered comatose then spirited
away to the "Jefferson Institute" (heavy irony in that name!)
where their brain-dead bodies are kept alive by mechanical
means to serve as a living black-market organ bank for the
ultimate benefit of the very wealthy. In Sphinx, archaeologist
Erica Baron uncovers a vicious underworld overseeing the theft
and sale of Egyptian antiquities. In Brain Dr. Martin Phillips
learns that women kidnapped after injection during gynecolog-
ical examinations are being used for bio-computer interface,
their bodies kept alive in big glass jars by a new kind of
villain, a mad computer scientist. They do not suffer because their pleasure centers are stimulated by electrically
induced orgasm.

> Philips made a slow complete circle around the cylinder.
> An awful weakness spread over him and his legs threatened
> to give way.
> "You probably know," said Michaels, "that significant
> advances in computer science, like feedback, came from
> studying biological systems. It's really what cybernetics
> is all about. Well, we've taken the natural step and gone
> to the human brain itself. . . . "We've studied it like
> any other vastly complicated machine. And we've succeeded,
> beyond our dreams. We've discovered how the brain stores
> its information, how it accomplishes parallel processing
> of information rather than the inefficient serial
> processing of yesterday's computers, and how the brain
> is organized in a functionally hierarchical system.
> Best of all, we've learned how to design and build a
> mechanical system that mirrors the brain and has these
> same functions. And it works, Martin! It works beyond
> your wildest imagination!"
> Michaels had nudged Philips to continue down the row of
> cylinders, looking in at the exposed brains of the young
> women, all at different levels of vivisection. . . .

> "Now, listen," said Michaels. "I know it's shocking when you first see it. But this scientific breakthrough is so big that it is inconceivable to contemplate the immediate benefits. In medicine alone, it will revolutionize every field. You've already seen what our very preliminary program will do with a skull X ray. Philips, I don't want you to make any snap decisions, you understand?"[5]

And finally in Fever biochemical researcher Charles Martel (he proves equal to his name) battles simultaneously to substitute immuno-therapy for the efforts of chemo-therapists who would actually kill his 14-year-old daughter in order to bring about a remission of her leukemia and the forces who would kill him to keep from coming to light the dumping of the up-river chemical plant whose criminal irresponsibility caused her disease.

Each of the three med-tech novels orbits about the image of a helpless human tormented, killed, or worse by combination of human greed and bureaucratic stupidity, attached to machinery against her will, machinery which serves as an emblem for an inefficient and often lethal bureaucracy. In each work the hero finds herself all but defeated by a bureaucracy evidently constructed for precisely that function. In Fever, it's the Environmental Protection Agency:

> . . . Charles went back to his desk and called the EPA General Information number. This time it was answered by a women with a bored Boston accent.
> Charles introduced himself and said he wanted to report serious dumping of poisonous material into a river.
> The woman was not impressed. She put Charles on hold.
> Another woman picked up, who sounded so similar to the first that Charles was surprised when she asked him to repeat his request.
> "You've got the wrong extension," said the woman. "This is the Water Programs Division and we don't handle dumping. You want the Toxic Chemical Program. Just a minute."[6]

Again put on hold, Charles finds the listing for the Toxic Chemical Program in the phone directory. An identical voice tells him they have nothing to do with infractions and tells him to call the number for Oil and Hazardous Material Spills. Reaching that number, he repeats his request.

> "When did the spill take place?" asked the woman.
> "This is continuous dumping, not a one-time accident."
> "I'm sorry," said the woman. "We only handle spills."
> "Can I speak to your supervisor?" growled Charles.
> "Just a minute," sighed the woman.

When Charles tries to explain to the supervisor that a factory is regularly dumping benzene (a deadly poison) into a local river, he is told he must call the proper state agency first.

"Okay," said the woman after hearing his problem. "What river are you talking about?"

"The Pawtomack," said Charles. "My God, am I finally talking to the right people?"

"Yes, you are," reassured the woman. "And where is the factory you think is dumping?"

"The factory is in Shaftesbury," said Charles.

"Shaftesbury?" questioned the woman. "That's in New Hampshire, isn't it?"

"That's right but . . ."

"Well, we don't handle New Hampshire."

"But the river is mostly in Massachusetts."

"That might be," said the woman, "but the origin is in New Hampshire. You'll have to talk to them."

Cook's decision to make his protagonist in Fever a man of heroic determination and fortitude is appropriate: the bureaucratic run-around lasts for days, takes Charles through a labyrinth of state and federal offices, and achieves almost nothing. Similar scenes occur in each book. It is important to interject here that Cook is not indicting the people in these bureaucracies but the system itself, which enslaves them just as it traps victims and threatens the hero. In the bureaucracy's miasmic depths, the evil schemes of irresponsible scientists grow like toadstools in a swamp.

Of course these books are exaggerated, but their exaggeration is extrapolative, not fantastic. In addition to the many real-world examples offered by Cook, we might add others as they come to light in the newspapers. After Coma, was published, for instance, the following report appeared on the front page of The Cincinnati Enquirer:

'WRONG GAS' SUSPECTED IN 5 DEATHS

NORRISTOWN, Pa. (AP) - Because nobody realized the pipes were mislabeled, oxygen was confused with "laughing gas" for six months at a hospital emergency room near here, officials said Tuesday. The hospital said the mixup may have caused five deaths.

Suburban General Hospital also said a total of 35 deaths were reported by the newly-built emergency room during that period, and state health officials said they were investigating whether the foul-up played a part in any. . . .

It was also disclosed that as many as 300 patients may have been given nitrous oxide instead of oxygen, or the reverse, between December 15, when the emergency room opened, and July 6, when the mixup was discovered. . . .

According to hospital officials, an anesthesiologist discovered the mistake while administering what he thought was oxygen to a drowning victim.

When the patient kept turning blue, the anesthesiologist hooked the patient to a portable oxygen tank and the discoloration disappeared.

The doctor then took about six deep breaths from the pipe labeled "oxygen" and discovered it was nitrous oxide.[7]

Why have there been no studies of Cook? Aren't we missing out on the important imaginative visions of a socially conscious writer of science fiction, a surgeon and teacher of opthalmology in his own right, incidentally? In the past decade a blizzard of academic papers has discussed in detail the criticism of bureaucratic institutions and overreliance on the mechanical in preference to the human in such horrific dystopian visions as The Machine Stops, by E. M. Forster, William Hjortsberg's Gray Matters, "Roller Ball Murder," basis for the film, Rollerball, THX-1138 (film by Lucas, novelization by Ben Bova), Harlan Ellison's "I Have No Mouth and I Must Scream," and Megan Terry's Home: Or Future Soap.[8] Less has been said, however, concerning works which are minimally or marginally science fiction but in which social criticism is for that very reason rendered all the stronger. A case in point is the recent film, The China Syndrome, which shows clearly what can be accomplished by way of social criticism with no extrapolation of technology but only a very short-term futuristic premise. Similarly, the disaster film, Rollover, in which economic collapse occurs should receive attention as science fiction, not because economics was once called the dismal science but because the film's imagined world-wide disaster renders it science fiction every bit as much as depictions of nuclear holocaust taking place in the near future. The critique in both works is similarly focused: The Sorcerer's Apprentice has tampered with forces he cannot control, creating an unresponsive, out-of-control entity (the bureaucracy or the weapon in the hands of one) with a life of its own whose very existence is a threat to all.

If we as a discipline are, as it appears, endlessly fascinated by the speculative fantasy which shakes the admonitory finger, should we not be at least mildly interested in that fiction of science, technology, and systems which shakes the angry fist? And if we answer in the negative, perhaps we should consider that the "ghetto walls" we have so long deplored may be largely created and sustained by ourselves, the insubstantial fabric of our own Santaroga Barrier.

Miami University

Notes

[1] An examination of the yearly bibliographies of the Science Fiction Research Association reveals no mention of Cook.

[2] The Science Fiction Encyclopedia, ed. Peter Nicholls (Garden City, NY: Doubleday, 1979).

[3] Earlier at this meeting Joe Debolt, Past President of the Science Fiction Research Association, suggested that one problem in the criticism of science fiction may be a kind of trendiness in choice of subjects for study; the title for the Earthsea article was offered in jest by Brian Aldiss at Boca Raton in 1980.

[4] In Explorers of the Infinite (Cleveland, Ohio: World Publishing Co., 1963), p. 11, Sam Moskowitz gave a definition of science fiction which serves us well in considering the

novels of Cook: "Science fiction is a branch of fantasy identifiable by the fact that it eases the 'willing suspension of disbelief' on the part of its readers by utilizing an atmosphere of scientific credibility for its imaginative speculations in physical science, space, time, social science, and philosophy." In Cook's novels, the scientists, hospitals, research labs, support staffs and administrations effect a near-total suspension of disbelief which eases acceptance of the fantastic elements in the conclusions of Cook's novels.

[5]Brain, (New York: G. P. Putnam's Sons, 1981), pp. 203-204.

[6]Fever, (New York: G. P. Putnam's Sons, 1982), pp. 120-121.

[7]The Cincinnati Enquirer, August 3, 1977, p. 1.

[8]Several other works and critiques of this type will be found in the "Annotated List of Works Useful for the Study of Mechanized Environments in SF" included in Clockwork Worlds: Mechanized Environments in SF (Richard D. Erlich and Thomas P. Dunn, eds.), appearing from Greenwood Press in 1983 as part of the series, Contributions to the Study of Science Fiction and Fantasy, under the general editorship of Marshall B. Tymn.

Richard D. Erlich

Moon-Watcher, Man, and Star-Child:
2001 as Paradigm

All of 2001: A Space Odyssey is divided into three parts.[1] Or, at least, it's divisible into three parts: the pre-human past, among our australopithecine ancestors; the human present in 2001 and a bit thereafter; and the human future in the Superman, Star-Child.
Back in the academic year of 1970-71 at the University of Illinois, I taught a writing course for biology majors in which we studied 2001, stressing its first part. We worked mostly on the way Arthur C. Clarke and Stanley Kubrick had taken the scientific theory of a predatory and weapons transition from ape to human and translated it into the fiction of "The Dawn of Man" section of the film and novel.[2] Since then, I have used the first part of 2001 in courses in science fiction, where we continue to look at how Clarke and Kubrick translated science into fiction and also look at the first part of the novel, and the novel as a whole, as an example of a First Contact story.
In 1978, I delivered a paper on science fiction perceptions of being "Trapped in the Bureaucratic Pinball Machine: A Vision of Dystopia in the Twentieth Century."[3] In my discussion of the image of people trapped in literal machines, I discussed the central part of 2001, where people are always in mechanized environments in the film, and almost always in mechanized environments in the novel. Then, in 1981, I spoke on "Immanence in Some Works by Ursula K. LeGuin, Contrasted with Transcendence in Some Works by A. C. Clarke."[4] And, in my discussion of Clarke, I covered the last section of 2001, the creation of Star-Child.
After that third essay, it only took me about four or five months to figure out that just about everything I was interested in in science fiction studies could be found in 2001: First Contact, how science is transformed into fiction, mechanized environments (with attempted computer-

takeover), and a wondrous journey ending in the transcendence of the human condition with the mystic creation of a Superman. Another month or so, and I figured out that 2001 deals with many of the things most people are interested in in science fiction--quite enough to take up a full semester's work of instruction on the undergraduate level.[5]

That the motif of First Contact is important in science fiction is a point that needn't be argued, certainly not in the year that saw the release of the re-make of The Thing and which is seeing Steven Spielberg's E.T. on its way to being the hottest item of mass culture since Rubik's Cube. And, certainly, one of the things science fiction is supposed to do, on occasion, is to translate science into fiction. Mechanized environments and computer-takeover have also been of some interest to writers and students of science fiction. Thomas P. Dunn's and my selected List of Works Useful for the Study of Mechanized Environments in science fiction runs, in manuscript, over 130 pages.[6] The marvelous journey is called by Northrop Frye, "the one formula ["of all fictions"] that is never exhausted"; and the Superman business has been canonized as an official Theme in The Science Fiction Encyclopedia, which lists over sixty works dealing with the subject. Finally, transcendence has been a major science fiction concern since at least Clarke's Childhood's End and continues strongly unto this day: the word "transcendent" and its cognates comprise a literal motif in the book reviews I have examined in the British journal Foundation.[8] So: First Contact, science into science fiction, mechanized environments, the wondrous journey and transcendence--all major parts of science fiction, and they are all intrinsic to 2001.

The First Contact motif was both explicit and familiar in Clarke's early versions of 2001, the ones published in his volume on The Lost World of 2001.[9] In the finished novel and, more so, in the film, the motif is subtle, since Clarke and Kubrick wisely chose never to show the extraterrestrials. What we see is the monolith or monoliths: the E.T.'s device and the "objective correlative" for them.[10] To some extent, we go to the mysterious monoliths. In the film this is stressed by the australopithecines', the humans' on the Moon, and Dave Bowman's all reaching out to a monolith.[11] To a much greater extent, however, the monoliths go to or summon us; we transcend our protohuman and human conditions by the E.T.'s grace.

This idea of "grace" is important for Clarke's idea of transcendence, and helps bring 2001, in good quest fashion, around in a kind of thematic circle, with the transcendence theme indirectly related to the initial First Contact of monolith and australopithecines and very directly related to 2001's ultimate First Contact (and the literal completion of Dave Bowman's odyssey): when Star-Child returns to Earth, and we humans meet the Superman. The science-into-fiction business is somewhat less interesting than man-becomes-god. Still, science is important for science fiction (so called), even if it may be less basic to science fiction (as practiced) than such basic myths as the serpent's strongest appeal to Eve: to be like God.

In The Lost Worlds of 2001, Clarke reprints his log entry

for October 2, 1964, where he notes finishing Robert Ardrey's African Genesis and being struck by the phrase, "a gift from the stars."[12] Clarke and Kubrick took from Ardrey his weapons-transition version of Raymond Dart's theory of "The Predatory Transition from Ape to Man" and present this transition as a very literal "gift from the stars."[13] What they did with the Dart-Ardrey theory--and with territoriality and other, less controversial anthropological and ethological lore--is what art generally does with theories. They took the theory, an abstraction, an "airy nothing," and gave it "a local habitation and a name"--or several names.[14] For the Australopithecinae we get Moon-Watcher and his tribe of starving man-apes. For territoriality, we get Moon-Watcher and his tribe pitted against the Others (capital "O") at the muddy stream. For the weapons transition, we get Moon-Watcher's murder of One-Ear, leader of the Others--and, in the film, that famous matched cut of Moon-Watcher's soaring bone weapon reaching its zenith, beginning to fall, and becoming a human-made satellite, moving through space. For Ardrey's polemics on Man (and it's always Man, the male, in all these works), on Man as essentially a violently territorial killer-ape, with recently acquired erect posture and enlarged brain--for Ardrey's polemics we get Clarke's ironic observation that human weapons' building and reproductive success have led us to a twenty-first century where we're again hungry and threatened with extinction. That's in the novel; in the film 2001, we get Kubrick's more Nietzschean theme of how the last men threaten to kill off our species with boredom.[15]

So much for the beginning of 2001. The middle section moves from the open savannahs of Africa to the vastness of space, where humans are, necessarily, enclosed within literal machines or at least are in the highly mechanized environments of Moon bases or space suits. We are protected by those machines and space suits and underground bases, but we are also confined and, ultimately, threatened by them.

As Gary K. Wolfe correctly insists, most spaceships in science fiction are more womb than phallus, and this holds true for all the mechanized environments in 2001.[16] But wombs just are not proper places for adults. The mechanized environments in 2001 stand poised between the dangerous African plains of the australopithecines and the "galactic gulfs" confidently crossed by Star-Child. Our mechanical wombs are necessary for us if we are to explore space--at this stage of our evolution; but this stage of evolution is precisely what we must transcend if we are to attain the stars. "The stars are not for Man," not even for humans with spacecraft, and we must transcend our machines and the machine-using phase of human development; we must break free of our mechanized environments.[17] This womb-threat is the primary meaning of the mechanized environments of 2001; and the motif comes through brilliantly in the film in Kubrick's images of mechanized confinement, with machines inside machines inside machines, all surrounding, enclosing, protecting, and confining human beings.

More conventional is the obvious threat of HAL 9000 when he becomes a killer. Clarke explains Hal's murders in terms of a neurosis induced by withholding truth from Dave Bowman and Frank Pohl. Kubrick is far less specific, relying on the decorum of Hal's becoming a killer and our conventional mistrust of overly-powerful computers and of any thinking entity that thinks itself incapable of error. In Kubrick's vision, humans and machines are very like one another, and in 2001 the essential human tools are weapons--and man is, essentially, a killer. It is decorous, then, that the ultimate tool, HAL 9000, should become a weapon; decorous that Hal, the most human character in the film, should become a murderer; decorous that a "roboticized" Dave Bowman should have to kill Hal to achieve full humanity; and decorous that Hal should be the one character in the film to suffer a fully human death.

The mechanized environments in the central part of 2001 fit in with the story's thematic concerns and also place 2001 into the dystopian and satiric tradition where people are diminished by our machines. Bowman's victory over Hal moves this section into the more optimistic tradition of science fiction where heroes finally defeat the machines; Bowman's victory and subsequent enlightenment about the true nature of his mission prepare us for 2001's conclusion, especially in the film, where the last word spoken is Dr. Floyd's final comment on TMA-1 as a mystery.[18]

The transcendent conclusion of 2001 fits in with the religious, mythic, and mystic concerns of much science fiction and is interesting when considered with such other "religious" science fiction as Robert A. Heinlein's Stranger in a Strange Land, Frank Herbert's Dune series, and LeGuin's radically different The Lathe of Heaven. The ending of 2001 is especially interesting when considered with Clarke's own Childhood's End.

In Childhood's End, we get the Eastern form of entering godhood, with the dissolving of the individual Self into the real reality of things. In Childhood's End, the Selves of Earth's children merge into a group mind, and eventually, and spectacularly, that group mind merges with the god-like Overmind. In 2001, we remain more in the Western mystic tradition, with Dave Bowman's maintaining his identity when he becomes Star-Child but still, paradoxically, being part of the E.T.s and in communion with them. In Childhood's End, the merged children of Earth leap up into the Overmind; in 2001, Dave Bowman travels out to meet the gods. In both Childhood's End and 2001, however, it is by the grace of the god-figures that humankind achieves our final apotheosis.[19] The Overmind must come to Earth for the children to join it; the E.T.s must "deify" Dave Bowman for him to join them.

Childhood's End and 2001 are very useful to teach together to undergraduates since most of them resist strongly the idea that, as descendants of Eve, they might have as a birthright the desire to "be like God," knowing the fullness of the universe as well as good and evil. They also view with horror the idea of loss of identity and absorption into a greater being. So the ending of 2001 is usually much more acceptable to them than that of Childhood's End. I advise teaching 2001 and Childhood's End along with excerpts from the biblical Book of Ecclesiastes and with Heinlein's short story, "They."[20] Koheleth (the Preacher in Ecclesiastes) and Heinlein's protagonist in "They" offer the rigorous Cynicism that shows why one might want godhead to avoid a life of both mechanical cycles and a rigid, railroad-track life leading from womb to tomb. Both show why one might prefer 2001's version of "The Myth of the Eternal Return," or Childhood's End's version of Nirvana, to the reality of being trapped in the mechanisms of a machine-universe or of machine civilization.21

As both film and novel--especially if one can teach both-- 2001 is pedagogically paradigmatic. It hardly contains every theme of science fiction (no work could do that), but it contains enough to structure several years of science fiction study. As both film and novel, 2001 shows us how science can be made into art and how such conventional material as First Contact, mechanized environments, computer-takeover, the wondrous journey, and mystic transcendence can be made into high art, indeed.

Miami University

Notes

1Stanley Kubrick, dir., 2001: A Space Odyssey, MGM, 1968, screenplay by Stanley Kubrick and Arthur C. Clarke; Arthur C. Clarke, 2001: A Space Odyssey (New York: New American Library, 1968), "based on a screenplay by Stanley Kubrick and Arthur C. Clarke." I shall not deal with the complex relationship between the making of 2001 as film and its writing as a novel, preferring to deal with 2001 as, essentially, one work of art: one story, told in film and in a novel. Only where absolutely essential to my argument will I point out the differences between the two works. Let the reader, however, beware: there are a large number of places where film and novel differ that I will not point out. The secondary literature on 2001 is daunting in its volume, and I have not reviewed most of it. Science fiction students made of sterner stuff should begin with The Making of Kubrick's 2001, ed. Jerome Agel (New York: New American Library, 1970) and Carolyn Geduld's Filmguide to 2001: A Space Odyssey (Bloomington and London: Indiana University Press, 1973). Agel excerpts a number of reviews of 2001 and offers a ninety-six page photo insert and other material of interest; Geduld's brief monograph includes a useful bibliography of critical works on the film. Geduld also usefully disagrees with me, stressing the four major episodes of 2001 as film; see pp. 5-8 and 34. For introductions to the fiction of A. C. Clarke, see George Slusser, The Space Odysseys of Arthur C. Clarke (San Bernardino: Borgo Press, 1978)--Slusser, correctly makes much of "transcendence" in Clarke; Arthur C. Clarke, ed. Joseph D. Olander and Martin Harry Greenberg (New York: Taplinger, 1977); and Eric S. Rabkin, Arthur C. Clarke, Starmont Reader's Guide 1 (West Linn, OR.: Starmont House, 1979)--Rabkin comments usefully on monoliths in Clarke's work and makes an interesting case for Clarke's view of the universe being "homocentric" (i.e., centered on humans).

2I have reported on this exercise in "Strange Odyssey: From Dart to Ardrey to Kubrick and Clarke," Extrapolation,

17 (May 1976), 118-24.

³In *Selected Proceedings of the 1978 Science Fiction Research Association National Conference*, ed. Thomas J. Remington (Cedar Falls: University of Northern Iowa, 1979), pp. 30-44.

⁴Paper delivered at the section on LeGuin's Short Fiction, 1981 Science Fiction Research Association National Conference, at Denver, June 1981.

⁵Working with more sophisticated students on the graduate level, I have been obliged to add science fiction bibliography, "hard" science science fiction, and space war; but, even on the graduate level, *2001* is sufficiently "paradigmatic" (taking that buzz word very broadly) to allow a teacher to organize a course around the broad themes of *2001* as film and novel.

⁶Richard D. Erlich and Thomas P. Dunn, eds., *Clockwork Worlds: Mechanized Environments in SF* (Westport, CT: Greenwood Press, in production).

⁷*Anatomy of Criticism: Four Essays* (1957; rpt. New York: Atheneum, 1966), First Essay, p. 57; *The Science Fiction Encyclopedia*, Peter Nicholls, gen. ed. (Garden City, NY: Doubleday, 1979), pp. [13] and 581-85.

⁸See also *The Science Fiction Encyclopedia*'s entries for "Computers," "Gods and Demons," and "Religion" (esp. p. 495).

⁹(New York: New American Library, 1972.)

¹⁰The monolith--or a monolity--contacts Moon-Watcher's tribe of australopithecines; the men on the Moon find TMA-1, the same or another monolith; a monolith leads (in the first part of the "trip" sequence in the film) or sends (in the novel) Dave Bowman on the most spectacular part of his odyssey; a monolith appears before Bowman to mediate his final transformation into Star-Child.

¹¹Bowman's gesture is rather like that of Adam in Michelangelo's *Creation of Man* on the ceiling of the Sistine Chapel. For an intriguing interpretation of the imagery of mystic marriage in Bowman's apotheosis--and for Bowman as a "sperm-figure"--see Donald Palumbo, "Loving that Machine; Or, The Mechanical Egg: Sexual Mechanisms and Metaphors in Science Fiction Films," *The Mechanical God: Macines in Science Fiction*, ed. Thomas P. Dunn and Richard D. Erlich (Westport, CT: Greenwood Press, 1982), Essay 11, esp. pp. 122-23.

¹²"True, Ardrey is talking about cosmic-ray mutations, but the phrase 'A gift from the stars' is strikingly applicable to our present plot line" (p. 34). Clarke quotes Robert Ardrey, *African Genesis* (1961; rpt. New York: Dell, 1963), Ch. 9, section 3, p. 261.

Notes

¹³Raymond Dart, "The Predatory Transition from Ape to Man," <u>International Anthropological and Linguistics Review</u>, 1 (1953), 201-19.

¹⁴See the comments on poets by that very poetical contemner of poetry, Shakespeare's Duke Theseus: <u>A Midsummer Night's Dream</u>, V.i.12-16.

¹⁵For Friedrich Nietzsche on the banality of the "last men," see his <u>Thus Spake Zarathustra</u>, Prolog, section 5. Kubrick "cites" Nietzsche by using Richard Strauss' <u>Also Sprach Zarathustra</u> at key points in the film, with Strauss' World-riddle theme becoming the theme of the Superman in the film, reaching its crescendo with Moon-Watcher's triumph over One-Ear, the appearance of Star-Child over the Earth--and with the name of Stanley Kubrick in the opening credits. For excellent comments on Kubrick's use of Nietzsche and Strauss, see the excerpt from John Allen's <u>Christian Science Monitor</u> review of <u>2001</u> in Agel, <u>The Making of Kubrick's 2001</u>, pp. 231-32 (see n.1).

¹⁶<u>The Known and the Unknown: The Iconography of Science Fiction</u> (Kent, OH: Kent State University Press, 1979), Ch. 3. For more on sexual imagery in <u>2001</u>, see C. Geduld, Filmguide and Palumbo, "Loving that Machine," n. 1 and n. 11, above.

¹⁷The quotation is from Clarke's <u>Childhood's End</u> (New York: Ballantine, 1953), Ch. 14, p. 137; see also Ch. 24, p. 212. To combine Gary K. Wolfe, A. C. Clarke, and Andrew Marvell, we might say, "The womb's a fine and comfy place, / But bad for progress of our race." See also Clarke's <u>The City and the Stars</u> (New York: Harcourt, Brace, 1956)--available in a Signet rpt. (New York: New American Library, 1957).

¹⁸In Kubrick's film of <u>2001</u>, we move from clear satire in the central section to the clearly mythic. This shift will not surprise students of N. Frye's <u>Anatomy of Criticism</u> (see n. 7). Frye says that science fiction "is a mode of romance with a strong inherent tendency to myth: and suggests that his five modes, moving from myth down to the ironic, or satiric, "evidently go around in a circle," with fully-developed satire moving toward "the reappearance of myth" (First Essay, pp. 49 and 42). Ignoring <u>Spartacus</u> (1959-60), Kubrick's films from, say, <u>Paths of Glory</u> (1957) through <u>2001</u> may show a movement from Frye's "low mimetic" (in a tragic form) through satiric to the mythic, perhaps recapitulating in miniature the broader pattern Frye has discovered in recent European literature. Certainly, I recall hearing the questions asked after <u>Dr. Strangelove</u>, Where can Kubrick go from here? Since "here," <u>Dr. Strangelove</u>, was and is a perfectly realized cinematic satire, it may be highly significant that Kubrick followed it with the mostly mythic <u>2001</u>: Frye's "Theory of Modes" may have predictive value.

¹⁹I discuss Clarke's theme of "grace descending" in my essay on "Immanence in Some Works by Ursula K. LeGuin, Contrasted with Transcendence in Some Works by A. C. Clarke,"

cited in n. 4.

[20] Robert A. Heinlein, "They," Unknown, April 1941 (magazine title changed to Unknown Worlds in Oct. of 1941-- Science Fiction Encyclopedia, "Unknown" entry, p. 621); rpt. frequently including Science Fiction: The Future, ed. Dick Allen (New York: Harcourt Brace Jovanovich, 1971) and Above the Human Landscape . . . , ed. Willis E. McNelly and Leon E. Stover (Pacific Palisades: Goodyear, 1972); collected in Heinlein's The Unpleasant Profession of Jonathan Hoag (Hicksville, NY: Gnome Press, 1959).

[21] I crib the quoted phrase from Mircea Eliade, The Myth of the Eternal Return; or, Cosmos and History, trans. Willard R. Trask (1954, corrected printing 1965; rpt. Princeton: Princeton University Press, 1971). Slusser stresses "transcendence and return" in his discussion of 2001 in Space Odysseys, pp. 57-60 (see n.1).

Jane Bloomquist and William McMillan

Science Fiction Theater the Moebius Way

Science fiction is a communal art form. If you doubt that fact try to board any hotel elevator while they host a convention. It has become a cliche that fans participate: young and old readers finance and publish their own "fanzines," write letters to the editors' columns in the "prozines," submit stories, and become "pros." Readers volunteer time and effort to hold local, regional, national, and world cons. Fans get together, form societies, create worlds and people them with wonderments. So it has been with Moebius Theatre. Moebius Theatre is a professional comedy theater which began as a science fiction fandom organization. As such, it is interesting as a study in theater, science fiction, and fandom. This paper studies the growth of the Moebius Theatre through an examination of their organizational structure and a thematic and performance criticism of four of their seminal productions.

The Moebius Theatre began when Michael Blake attended "Big Mac," the Thirty-fourth World Science Fiction Convention in 1976. One of the convention highlights was to have been a full-scale professional theater production based on Cordwainer Smith's <u>Lords of the Instrumentality</u>. The program book proudly proclaimed, "The play will be a completely professional production utilizing the talents of the best professional theatrical talents in Kansas City, with elaborate sets, costumes, and effects."[1] The production failed. It failed to live up to its claim of professionalism, and it failed to keep the audience's interest. It was too big. The script attempted to interweave six additional stories by other authors and still maintain Smith's main thread of action. The setting, costuming, and lighting tried physically to recreate Smith's imaginative world. In trying to provide everything it gave nothing. Michael Blake was heard to boast that even he could do better. His friends around him agreed. Shortly after the convention they formed

Moebius Theatre.

For several years Moebius existed as a loosely structured performance group operating under Blake's leadership. In 1980 he stepped down to be replaced by Charles Ott and later Marty Coady became and is still president of the group. Moebius Theatre now operates as a chartered, not-for-profit corporation in the state of Illinois. The president is assisted in her duties by four governors. The corporation is democratic in its operations and offers copyright privileges for itself and its members.

Moebius has maintained its communal, almost familial, identity by operating, as most fan societies do, out of a member's living room. Many of the original Moebians are still active, but over the years Blake estimates that as many as forty-five people have been involved. All Moebians, however, were readers of science fiction and fans before they joined the group. There are approximately twenty-five active members currently in the group. The greater number of them hold university degrees and work in fields of advanced technology.

The Moebians currently meet every Wednesday evening. Performances are critiqued and possibilities for future productions are discussed. New scripts are read aloud. The group then engages in a critical discussion of scene analysis and character development and makes suggestions for changes, deletions, and additions. The author or other Moebians will then revise and rewrite the script. Except for Moebius' first show all of their scripts have been original and most of them have been subjected to group polishing sessions before being added to the repertory.

Rehearsals tend to take place on Wednesdays after meetings and on Fridays and Sundays. Casting is always open, but few new people come to audition. Most casting is done in a rather relaxed fashion from within according to who has the time and desire to perform. Directors and producers of productions are Moebius participants who express interest and demonstrate abilities in these areas. Many Moebians write, perform, direct, and produce. Most Moebians double as technicians. A very important directorial function is to make the experience enjoyable for everyone. Heavy-handed approaches do not work well in the loosely structured, familial atmosphere Moebius Theatre is designed to create.

Most of the Moebius material takes the form of what they call "bits," short comic pieces with minimal technical requirements. Although all of these bits are original, many satirize familiar science fiction names, places, and situations; some borrow directly from published stories; and a few are direct parodies. Parodies are very popular, but Moebius prefers to do original work believing that parodies have only a transitory effect upon the audience and become immediately dated. The Moebius bits are preserved in an ever-growing portfolio entitled Wholly Babel. There are currently about twenty-two structured groups of bits and complete shows which are repeated with variations and some new material. Most bits have introductions which are rewritten for such audience. Introductions are scripted and rehearsed but are usually given off-stage. Only recently were authors' names added to the Wholly Babel table of contents. When they decided to begin giving authorial credit there was much good natured confusion over who had done which draft. To compound the confusion there were many bits which had been generated out of group interaction and improvisation.

In addition to the bits, Moebius has also performed four full-length original comedies. The group wrote <u>Stage Wars</u>: <u>Or Who's Biggs</u>?. Chuck Ott contributed <u>Parking Orbit</u> and <u>Spark</u>. Paul Gadzikowski wrote the one-act <u>Better Late Than Never</u>. Like the bits, these scripts are comedies featuring science fiction themes.

What is science fiction and what are science fiction themes? Those questions have been debated for quite some time, and I doubt we'll resolve them in this paper. James Gunn, in his authoritative <u>Alternate Worlds</u>: <u>The Illustrated History of Science Fiction</u>, provides a workable response to those questions, however, and we shall use his work as our paradigm in the study of the Moebius scripts.

James Gunn says, "In science fiction a fantastic event or development is considered rationally."[2] Frequently, though not always, science fiction features scientific discoveries without which the story would not take place. Mr. Gunn lists fourteen thematic categories for science fiction.[3] It is interesting and instructive to note that of Gunn's list of fourteen, the large majority of Moebius scripts deal with only four categories. They are: "Far Traveling" (changing the scene), "The Wonders of Science" (changing the tools), "Progress" (change itself, satirical), and "Man and Alien" (changing the cast). Together these four categories represent thirty-three of the fifty Moebius scripts we studied. Furthermore, there are no scripts representing the categories "Man and the Future" (change itself, plausible), "Superman" (as a new genus), or "Man and Religion" (changing man's beliefs). Clearly, science fiction as practiced by Moebius is concerned with man's confrontation with aliens and new worlds and with the wonders of science and progress.

The first Moebius performance took place one short month after "Big-Mac." Michael Blake was of the opinion that one of the reasons the production based on <u>Lords of the Instrumentality</u> failed was that it did not appeal to the imagination of the science fiction fan. The big sets and lavish costumes could never compete with the images the imagination of a well-read science fiction fan generates. Blake stripped the theatre performance down to its essentials: the actors and the script. Like most beginning ensembles, Moebius really didn't have the financial wherewithal to do big budget shows, but this wasn't strictly a money decision. As they have grown they have not changed this policy. They have found that when they begin to deal with any more than essential props and scenery they lose their special creative interplay with their audience.

Moebius' first performance was in Chicago at Windycon III. As has proved to be typical, the room was a standard hotel meeting room with a slightly raised platform at one end. The costuming was basic black and the props and set pieces were simple and kept to the minimum. The only lighting was that provided by the hotel for the room's normal use. A microphone was used to introduce the playlets and blackouts followed. The introductions and blackouts have become standard Moebius practice.

The performance consisted of three science fiction stories which, for the most part, were written in the form of a dialogue. In Mack Reynold's "The Business, As Usual," a time-traveler gets huckstered by a future version of the archtypic con man. Roger Zelazny's "Collector's Fever" features an alien rocklike life form which "deebles" for reproduction and an unfortunate prospective assassin who is too close for survival when deebling occurs. "Fun With Your New Head," by Thomas Disch, presents a barker hawking the latest in extra body parts. The audience was vocal in their approval, and thus reinforced, the Moebians committed themselves to future productions.

Moebius Theatre's fourth show brought them their first wide-ranging critical and popular success. The entire group wrote <u>Stage Wars: Or Who's Biggs?</u> which was first performed for Windycon IV. <u>Stage Wars</u> parodies <u>Star Wars</u>: Princess Layoff Organza seeks the help of Oke Wan Fenoke and Luke Warmwater in keeping Dumb Waiter, Grand Off-Target, and their Debtstar from foreclosing on the rebel planet. With the help of ME-2 ME-2, E-I-E-I-O, Drum Solo, D-owacka, and the Dead-eye Knights, the rebels succeed in their attempt to avoid foreclosure. <u>Stage Wars</u> followed hot on the heels of the popular movie and featured a tight script that played well. It was also able to include many ingags that only devoted fans would recognize. For instance, the "Biggs" of the subtitle refers to a character who appeared with Luke in a scene which was cut from the movie before its release. Only a single reference to the mysterious "Biggs" remains in the film. A large section of the Windycon IV audience, however, had read the original novel, and the answer to the question posed by the subtitle spread quickly through the crowd. At the Fortieth World Science Fiction Convention in Chicago Lucas Films revealed that Biggs will at last appear in <u>Revenge of the Jedi</u>.

The one-hour performance made extensive use of theatrical convention. The costumes were replicas of those used in the film, props were mimed, sets were minimal, the vaunted special effects of the movie were theatrically presented through the use of two actors who crossed the stage while carrying signs reading "Special Effect," and the fifteen member cast played approximately forty-five roles. The result was hilarious.

The performance was given in one of the hotel meeting rooms. Once again, lighting was determined by availability. Backstage organization was lacking, and the number of costume changes required by the small cast playing a large number of roles led to long blackouts and other technical delays. The script and the various performances were so well received, however, that the technical difficulties went unnoticed by all except the Moebius Theatre members.

Moebius repeated <u>Stage Wars</u> at Chambanacon in March 1978. That performance employed nineteen actors, and the four additional personnel reduced the number of quick changes and improved the backstage organization and technical efficiency of the production. Moebius received many other invitations to repeat this show, but Blake felt that the group should continue to work on original material and should refrain from relying upon the popularity of parodies. This was a brave decision for a newly formed theater group to make. It represented a commitment to the development of the group's talent and a rejection of the temptation to produce what sold well on the popular market.

Charles Ott's Spark, another seminal Moebius production, was first performed in 1981 at Capricon I in Evanston, Illinois, and represented a further extension of Moebius Theatre's development. Spark is a full-length play in two acts. It is the first script performed by Moebius that has extensive character development and plot lines. The theme of the play is "Man and Society" (change itself, descriptive), and it is developed through a story centering around the impact of a star-traveling culture upon a primitive, agrarian culture. Vantage Point, a planet outside the empire's galaxy, is the prime location for the four-hundred-year-long galactic mapping project. The story begins as the effort comes to a close and the citizens of Vantage Point begin to think of what their lives will be like after the departure of the star-traveling Observers.

The plot features a love quadrangle. Lord Algen is the foppish Observer in charge of the mapping project; a peasant girl, Cortay, has an adolescent crush on the sophisticated Algen; and a young Provider man, Benner, is in love with Cortay. Benner, armed with only a simple telescope and his self-trained intellect, has discovered an error in the Observers' galactic map. He is tempted to let the Observers leave without informing them of their mistake so that he might have Cortay to himself. He cannot, however, reconcile his desire with his conscience. Benner informs the Observers of their mistake, and though they first scoff at his claim, the Observers eventually realize their error. While Benner's scientific evaluations prove correct, his assumptions concerning Lord Algen's affections for Cortay prove unfounded. Lord Algen, it is discovered, is drawn to Grandmother Gill, supplier of foodstuffs, because she proves herself the only other person from either group to share both the "feet planted solidly on the ground" realism of the Providers and the cosmic vision of the Observers. We witness Algen drop his foppish persona as the relationship between him and Grandmother Gill develops.

Act II, Scene I, is a traditional character development scene where the foppish Lord and the aged food seller are shown to be more fully rounded persons than we might at first have thought:

> Algen: It [the galaxy] is so beautiful it is terrible. It looks like a fire, a raging forest fire burning the world away. And our whole system, this star and this planet and the Observatory all together, look like nothing more than a little glowing spark drifting up from that fire, ready to wink out as it cools. It's so beautiful that everything you are or might ever be looks squalid by comparison. Down here at least the daylight comes to hide it. Up in space it never does. . . .
> Grandmother Gill: I spend so much time under the light of the Galaxy I sometimes think I ought to get tan from it. I think it would be a different kind of tan, if there

were such a thing. It would be a tan that would make you shine from the inside, instead of getting darker, eh?[4]

The power of Spark lies in its characterizations; it belies the claim that science fiction is too interested in gadgets. Ott and Moebius have contributed a major work to science fiction theater.

To assist the actors in what is essentially a period play, Ott wrote a comprehensive historical background and extensive technical notes. He included a quote from Manners and Movements in Costume Plays to instruct the actor playing Algen in the proper method of taking snuff. In addition, Ott related in an interview that the single set locale of Spark was by design. Moebius' production of his Parking Orbit was complicated by several scene changes. Ott felt that there was a limit to how technical a science fiction theater production could become. With Parking Orbit in mind, Ott wrote Spark to be technically simple. Ott agreed with Blake that science fiction theater should rely upon the audience's ability to create the imaginative world within which the playwright and performers could house the action of the play. Pegasus Players, a professional theater production company in Chicago, selected Spark for its 1980 season, and it ran for a short time. Ott, however, was dissatisfied. He felt that one of the main problems with the Pegasus production was that the director did not understand the necessity of engaging the audience's imagination in the creation of the alternate world. Once again, a professional theater tended to over-produce the play. Because of this and other reasons Mr. Ott pulled Spark out of Pegasus.

Moebius Theatre's performance history spans six years, eight states, and approximately fifty productions at conventions, bars, colleges, video taping sessions, and professional theater houses. In May 1982, Moebius made their professional debut at The Theatre Shoppe in Chicago. They played for five weekends. They were scheduled to perform at The Organic Theatre, a Chicago Equity house, in November 1982. In June 1982, Moebius began a regular monthly performance at The Ginger Man, a theater-bar in Chicago. Their first Ginger Man show will be examined as representative of Moebius' professional performances.

The script for The Ginger Man was a compilation of bits from the Wholly Babel arranged in two acts with a running gag tying each act together. The running gag is used to lend continuity, sustain interest, and unify the performance. Blake credits television's "Ernie Kovac's Show" for this typical Moebius format. For this production, Moebius selected thirteen bits, seven for Act I and six for Act II. The thirteen bits and two running gags represent eight of the twelve thematic categories covered by Moebius scripts.

In Act I the three-part running gag was "My Buddy, My Car," a "Man and Machine" story about a computerized car that snitches on its drunken driver, is disconnected, and later takes revenge on its owner by locking him inside. This bit plays on the famous science fiction story and film, 2001: A Space Odyssey, by Arthur C. Clark and Stanley Kubrick. In the Moebius bit, the computer is Dave and the driver is Hal. Where the disconnected spaceship computer

reverted to singing its first-learned song, "A Bicycle Built
For Two," the disconnected automobile computer sings,
"Wouldn't you really rather have a Buick?" eventually running
down to "a Bu-iiickk."[5] A popular bit in this act was
"Forty-Four," a "Superpowers" story about a child with
super mental powers. The title derives from a little joke
the youngster plays on the scientist. While using a binary
system, she counts to the number forty-four (really 132)
on her fingers so that the number coincides with her raised
middle finger on each hand.

The running gag in Act II was the four-part "Martian
Pioneer Spacelines" based on the theme "Far Traveling." In
the gag a passenger is subjected to such terrors as a
strangling spacesuit, a revitalization unit demonstration
which proves nearly fatal, a star-crazed captain, and a
carnivorous strain of oxygen producing super-algae. "One
Afternoon in the Dark Ages," a "Wonders of Science" bit in
Act II, is an after the bomb story. A queen seeks knowledge
of the machines of the Ancients. A goat girl brings her such
prizes as a pocket calculator, a cassette tape recorder, and
a water-pik. The comic interpretations of the uses of the
machines eventually allow the goat girl to take control of
her society. The machines of the Ancients prove they still
retain their powers even if no one is quite sure what they
are.

The Ginger Man has a very small, slightly raised stage at
one end of a rectangular room filled with tables, chairs, and
a bar. The backstage area is a simple closet. The limita-
tions imposed by the backstage area caused traffic problems
which interfered with the flow of the production. In addition,
there was a lack of physicalization and follow-through in
mimed business. One of the main topics of discussion at the
next Moebius meeting was how to best deal with these difficulties for future shows at The Ginger Man and elsewhere. The
group confronted the problems and generated suggestions for
improving the performance much as they work together to improve their scripts.

Moebius Theatre is an ever-growing entity as evidenced by
the group, its literature, and its productions. Moebians did
not begin as theater artists but as fans; they have learned
by doing. They did not start with a set philosophy of performance or of literature. Rather they have evolved organical-
ly and have developed a vision and a style of their own. The
group, begun as a loosely structured fan organization, is now
incorporated. Its comic, dramatic literature is original with
new material appearing regularly. Productions are constantly
critiqued in order to hone the increasing number of performances.

Moebius' style of performance is distinctively classical.
The reliance upon the power of the word and the imagination
and knowledge of the audience hearkens back to the performance-
stage-audience relationship of the Elizabethans and the
text-audience unity of the Restoration. Moebius has con-
sistently shied away from attempting realistically to portray
the imaginative worlds created by their playwrights. Working
upon modified thrust or apron stages, Moebius has used very
little, if any, scenery and minimal or mimed props. In this
they are akin to the Elizabethans who worked upon the open

platform stage. Peter Brook has noted that the bare stage "enabled the dramatist effortlessly to whip the spectator through an unlimited succession of illusions, covering, if he chose, the entire physical world."[6] Moebius covers the entire physical world and beyond. The bare stage provides two additional primary benefits. First, it engages the imagination of the audience, reminding them of the performance nature of the event and making them partners in the creation of the production. Second, as Brook also noted, the bare stage allows the dramatist "free passage from the world of action to the world of inner impressions."[7] Grandmother Gill's comments on the light of the galaxy would become ludicrous if given before a painted drop, canvas flat, or gobo-lit cyclorama; and the audience would be impeded from empathizing with the character or appreciating her glowing tan.

Ray Bradbury has dabbled in playwriting and has written about his science fiction plays. He speaks about the importance of language and illusion or magic. Bradbury notes, "The two [language and illusion] come together and fuse in my science-fiction plays."[8] Bradbury has produced his own plays quite successfully and recommends a Shakespearean or Oriental simplicity in production: "Little scenery, few props, and an immense enthusiasm for myth, metaphor, language to win the day. In a science-fiction play, the harder you try to create the world of the future, the worse your failure."[9] Moebius Theatre has discovered this truth for themselves.

Moebius Theatre--indeed all science fiction theater--is, in many ways, a close relative of Restoration theater. When Charles II was restored to the throne of England in 1660, he reinstituted an art which had been forbidden for eighteen years. Most of the theaters had been burned down, and actors and dramatists had not worked in public since 1642. Charles II's court produced a new drama. The first dramatists of this period came from the nobility. Their audiences frequently numbered no more than sixty people, but among these were the king, visiting royalty, and various dukes, duchesses, earls, lords, and ladies of the court. Never before had there been so small or so elite an audience. The early Restoration dramatist wrote of and for this audience, and he wrote only comedies. The substance of their theater was, of course, completely different from that of science fiction theater, but the communicative power gained by the common knowledge and focus of interest shared by dramatist and audience is remarkably similar in Restoration and science fiction theater. Moebius continually relies upon the knowledgability of their audiences, leaning upon extended introductions when playing before mundanes, but for fan audiences frequently performing extended variations of science fiction themes and situations and frequently engaging in free-spirited improvisation.

Michael Blake, in his paper entitled "Black Hole Meets Blackout," elaborates upon Moebius Theatre's improvisational comedy. He notes, "The common denominator of both science fiction and improv is imagination--on the part of the artist, and on the part of the audience. As such, both science fiction and improv have a sort of elitist appeal."[10] Although most of Moebius' work is scripted, Blake's point is well taken. Many of their scripts grow out of improv, and many of their performances before fans are characterized by improv extensions. Successful comedy, in addressing the mind, requires an intelligent audience. The Restoration playwright, George Meredith, wrote, "There are plain reasons why the Comic poet remains without a fellow. A society of cultivated men and women is required, wherein ideas are current, and the perceptions quick, that he may be supplied with matter and the audience."11 For Moebius Theatre, science fiction supplies the matter and fandom supplies the matter and fandom supplies the audience.

>   Fans are we.
>   What more can be said?
>   We do it for price
>   And not for the bread.12

Northwestern University

Notes

[1] MidAmerican Program Book (Kansas City: Nickeledoon Graphic Arts Service, 1976), p. 26.

[2] James Gunn, Alternate Worlds: The Illustrated History of Science Fiction (Englewood Cliffs, N.J.: Prentice Hall, 1975), p. 32.

[3] Gunn, pp. 242-43.

[4] Charles Ott, Spark, TS, pp. 25-26.

[5] David Ihnat, "My Buddy, My Car," in Wholly Babel, TS, p. 161.

[6] Peter Brook, The Empty Space (Middlesex: Penguin Books 1976), p. 97.

[7] Brook, p. 97.

[8] Ray Bradbury, The Wonderful Ice Cream Suit and Other Plays (New York: Bantam Books, Inc., 1972), p. x.

[9] Bradbury, p. xi.

[10] E. Michael Blake, "Black Hole Meets Blackout," TS, p. 5.

[11] George Meredith, "On Comedy and the Uses of the Comic Spirit," in Comedy: Plays, Theory, and Criticism, ed. Marvin Felheim (Chicago: Harcourt Brace Jovanovich, 1962),

p. 206.

[12] This popular fan poem of unknown origin is quoted from Marty Coady.

Phyllis J. Day and Nora G. Day

Freaking the Mundane: A Sociological Look at
Science Fiction Conventions, and Vice Versa

According to Nicholls, science fiction fandom is "The active readership of science fiction and fantasy, maintaining contacts through fanzines and conventions."[1] Thus just to read science fiction is not enough to make one a part of fandom. Rather, it is necessary to identify oneself as a part of the fan group to others of like mind, through correspondence or attendance at the many science fiction conventions held around the nation. In addition, it is important to note that fandom is not simply a hobby, in the way readers of romances, westerns, and so on use recreation time for reading. "Fandom is not normal hobbyist group. It has been suggested that if science fiction in some way ceased to exist, fandom would continue to function quite happily without it."[2]

Fandom can, in fact, be classed as an American sub-culture. It has a tradition and history, its own language, and the members of fandom share " . . . values and beliefs and abide by norms that are, to varying degrees, different from those held by the majority."[3] Moreover, fandom had some of the characteristics of a religious cult--a " . . . mutual affirmation and sense of identity. . . . In Wallace's terms [communal cult institutions act as] rituals of intensification."[4] There is in fandom a consciousness of folk and the ritual of mass meetings. What fandom lacks as a cult is a charismatic leader and, perhaps, a central ideology, though one might well argue that the insistance on individuality and freedom of thought is the central ideology of fandom. Our sociological identification of fandom is, then, that it is a primarily American subculture which is paracultic in nature.

It is the purpose of this paper to look at science fiction conventions and fandom. We would like to discuss the characteristics of fen, some of their beliefs, the reasons they give for going to conventions, and then to make observations on science fiction fandom and its place in our society. A short glossary: "fen" is the plural of fan; "cons" are conventions; "mundanes" are those people not a part of fandom; "fiawol" is "fandom is a way of life."

We have, in the past year, gathered data via questionnaire and participant observation at science fiction conventions throughout the Midwest. Our survey was informational only for we believe that the value of such research lies in the accumulation of data from which hypotheses arise through grounded theory. It is our intention here to report to you on the people who belong to fandom and what they find in fandom that they do not find in the general culture. A few caveats are in order. First, our research was done only in Midwest conventions. It may be that those in the south, east, or west of the United States are markedly different. Secondly, sociologists may question the validity of the questionnaire data. Knowing the intense individuality of fen, we tried to word and order the questionnaire so that respondents had to place themselves in categories--we used, generally, three-point rather than five-point scales; and for some researchers this might not be "scientific enough. Also, we are very well aware that fen are playful people. That is not to say they do not tell the truth, but they do sometimes take things in more humor than was intended. We are sure that, with nearly 700 respondents, we have fairly good data. Some people played games, we know, but we feel from comments on the questionnaires from respondents that most did take the research seriously. Those questionnaires which very obviously were in fun we deleted from the quantifiable data but kept for participant observation data--for example, we did not quite believe a green dragon replied seriously.

Self-selection may create another bias. Questionnaires were placed near the registration tables to be picked up by choice of respondent. Although we received nearly 700 responses, we have no way of knowing why this group decided to respond while others did not, nor if the characteristics of our responding group are any real indication of the total population at conventions. Finally, we identify ourselves as fen. While we have tried to be objective, we do realize the bias this may create.

****

In the Midwest, there is at least one con within driving distance every month. Cons are held in hotels, many of which hold the same convention year after year. In summer and early fall, the addicted fan can often find two or three cons a month. They occur on weekends, beginning about noon on Fridays and winding down with "Dead Dog Parties" late on Sunday afternoons. Some cons are heavily programmed, with seminars on writing, creating science fiction cultures, the work of a particular author, or topics of general interest to fandom--outer space exploration, witchcraft, parapsychic phenomena, costuming, and so on. Even at "relaxicons" there is usually an attempt at programming--a few topics of interest are offered, in case anyone is interested. At these last, however, fen are more likely just to get together to talk with old friends, meet a few new ones, sing, and discuss whatever is of interest at the moment.

All the cons we attended had huckster rooms, or at least a space where people could display and sell their own work, art, gadgets, perhaps herbs and teas, crafts such as jewelry, and so on. In addition, people sell books, new or used, display new developments in computer technology, sell costumes, science fiction paraphernalia, or whatever they wish. Tables are rented by the hucksters, and the proceeds from rental help support the con.

Another feature is the art auction. There is a gallery of art done by fen, some of which is offered for sale outright and some of which will be auctioned. The auction usually occurs on Saturday night, with a small percentage of proceeds going to the con, the rest to the artists. Beautiful and unusual original work is available at these auctions, and at very reasonable prices.

Filksinging at cons can go on all night. Fen who have composed new music or "filked" old tunes and given them new, science fiction-oriented words are in attendance, along with people who play guitars and lead the singing and a changing audience of participants who drop in and stay a while or stay all night. As the night progresses, and good spirits of all kinds flow freely, filksings get bawdier and/or more lachrymose but never rowdy. Fen are usually very careful not to let that happen, as it would result in bad press with the hotel and community.

Costumes and the costume party are major features of most cons. The fen assume "personae," some of which are taken from science fiction and fantasy books or movies, some from historical periods, and some just from the minds of fen. We have barbarians in loin cloths (with fur bras for the women), men and women Transylvanian transvestites from the "Rocky Horror Picture Show," warriors from "Battlestar Galactica" and technicians from Star Trek. There are Wookies, little Fuzzies, witches and sorcerers, bug-eyed monsters, dragon riders, Jedi Masters, Dorsai "protectors," aliens of all kinds. One costume show, in particular, we must mention. There was a creature with the head of the alien from the movie "Alien" who, with serape and Mexican hat, won the humorous category with its "Illegal Alien" entry. There are swordspersons and futuristic warriors of all kinds, including the amazing almost-naked female fighters. Elves, gnomes, fairies, and Middle Earth Folk are seen everywhere.

Of course, not everyone wears a costume, and that is all right too. But the costumes are wonderful to see, well-crafted, and very interesting. Fen often maintain their costumed personae throughout the duration of the con, and dearly love to "freak the mundane" by going into the hotel restaurants, stalking the halls, or expanding outwards to the local McDonald's or Wendy's.

A special group of personae are those members of the Society for Creative Anachronism who overlap as fen. They are generally medieval knights, barons, lords and ladies, sorcerers, and people of that ilk. While swords and knives (and such weapons as laser pistols) must remain under peace bond (in holsters or scabbards fastened shut) while at cons, they are still much in evidence. Given the pacificistic nature of the fen in general, the display of such weapons is an anomaly.

Often there is a game room, in which people play Dungeons and Dragons or other fantasy games. Computer games may be set up, and fen have been known to remain attached to one video game almost throughout the whole con. Card games are not unusual, and one enterprising author finances his trips to cons with his "Memorial Seminar on the Redistribution of Wealth by Chance and Skill"--an institution at Midwest cons.

A note on authors--there are always a few at the cons. Some are invited to speak, some are invited just to be there, all are welcome, and many come just to hang around with people who like what they do. A very few are paid for their presentations, but this does not seem to be the mode. It is important also to note that these people are not held in awe by fen. Perhaps this is because many fen expect to write or are writing science fiction and fantasy and look upon the authors as "successful colleagues." There are, of course, a few groupies, and some authors who seek out groupies, but this does not seem to be a major factor.

Another feature at cons are the movie and/or video rooms. Depending on the size of the con, it may be possible to spend the entire weekend--day and night--watching movies, short features by fen, bloopers, or television video tapes. Movies range from the really atrocious, such as "Galaxina" or the "Astrozombies" to such fine films as "2001: A Space Odyssey" or "Wicker Man." Video tapes include special segments of "Star Trek" or "Battlestar Galactica," or old tapes to laugh at from "Lost in Space" or even "Father Knows Best." Bugs Bunny "carnivals" or foreign cartoons may be shown, as well as classic horror movies such as "Phantom of the Opera" or "Frankenstein--The True Story." "The Attack of the Killer Tomatoes" is a perennial at cons, as is the student-made film "The Thing that Ate Garganzola State University."

On Saturday night, before the costume judging, there is usually a banquet. Guests of honor who are writers speak, as do Fan Guests of Honor--those who have made contributions to the world of fandom itself. Banquets are catered by the hotel, and usually the main dish is fried chicken, baked chicken, chicken divan, or something of that sort--known to fandom banquet goers as "rubber chicken." Once, to our knowledge, "rubber ham" was served, but that was unusual fare. In addition to the speeches, there may be entertainment, perhaps a madrigal choir from a local college, or jugglers, magicians, and so on. There are rarely comedians, unless you want to count the authors.

The "con suite" is available for fen almost round the clock although some hotels limit con suite hours. Here fen sit to talk, drink free soft drinks or booze, hang around, sometimes sleep, or eat whatever is handy--snacks or food furnished by the Convention Committee or by fen who just bring food in. Conversations are rarely trivial--this is one of the most important observations of the research. They concern the effects of economics and politics on ecology, perhaps, or the place of space colonization in our future. Alternate societies, feminism, witchcraft as a healing religion, and of course the social meanings of particular science fiction and fantasy stories, are among the topics. The conversations are serious, in-depth, and, because of the intellectual characteristics of fen, often quite erudite. They can also be very funny or bawdy for fen are playful folk. One does not have to know someone to be included in group or conversation--just have enough interest to join in. And, of course, though the con suite is a general center for such discussions one finds them throughout the convention.

****

Of the nearly 700 people who filled out our questionnaires, 45% were women. Since fandom has the reputation of being mostly composed of white middle-class men, this is an unusual result. A note on the question asked of respondents: fen criticized us for asking for "gender" rather than "sex." Although we know the difference, we also knew that if we had asked "sex" of respondent, most would have answered "yes," or "occasionally," or "as often as possible." We nipped it in the bud.

Most fen are Caucasian. Black, Asian American, Native American, or other counted as less than 2% each. This verifies our observations. Although there were more members of minorities present in northern-most cons, probably there were no more than five or six non-Caucasians at any one convention. The lack of non-Caucasian fen probably mirrors the very few non-Caucasian writers and, perhaps, the readership of science fiction/fantasy.

Ninety-four percent of respondents were under the age of 40. Of these, 47% were between the ages of 20 and 29. One hundred forty-six people were below 21 years of age, and seven were above age 50. The youngest respondents were age 13, the oldest age 57. Sixty-five percent have some college education, and about 30% bachelor's degrees. Many respondents are still students. Another 18% have post graduate degrees, including 3% with doctorates. Seventeen percent have had no college, but of course many are too young (20% are below age 21). It is interesting to note that 52% of all respondents had high marks in secondary schools, and another 17% considered themselves average or above. Seventy-three percent of the respondents are single. Only 2.2% listed their sexual preference as homosexual, while 5.7% are bisexual.

About 27% were students, either at high school or college levels. Approximately 38% are in professional occupations such as teaching, social work, or computer-connected work. About 10% of all respondents had some connection with either the soft- or hardware of computer technology. Slightly under that number are librarians. Approximately 75% feel that they are middle income and above, though only 40% list incomes of $15,000 or more. Eight percent have incomes of more than $40,000 per year, and 22% did not show income.

Political beliefs carry out the image of fen as liberal and free thinking individualists. Only about 16% consider themselves conservative or at the radical right in politics. Sixty-six percent call themselves moderate or liberal, with another 12% nearing radical left or anarchist. Sixty-eight percent have no political affiliation, while 13% more are Democrats and 11% are Republicans. Only 17% did not vote in the 1980 elections--again many are students too young to vote. About 16.5% voted for Reagan, 21% for Carter, 31% for Anderson, and about 6% for others. Of the voting Democrats, 8% voted for Reagan, 58% for Carter and 31% for Anderson. Of Republicans, 56.5% voted for Reagan, while 7.2% voted for Carter and 26% for Anderson.

Fen categorize themselves in religious beliefs in the following manner. Thirty-seven percent considered themselves to be atheists or agnostic. About 41% belonged to no organized religion, and of the remainder 20% were practicing religionists. Of that group, 29% were Catholic, 53% Protestant, and 12% Jewish. One of the most surprising outcomes of the study was that approximately 19% of the respondents believe in witchcraft as a religion, and of these 8% practice it. Approximately 15% of the respondents considered themselves to be pagan or neo-pagan, and this number included many of the witches.

We asked that respondents identify the extent to which they were humanists and feminists, leaving the definitions of those terms to them. Of those responding to the humanist question, 49% said they were very much humanist while another 46% believed they were somewhat humanist. Many did not like the fact that we did not define what "humanist" meant, and said so in varying degrees of politeness. As to feminism, 43% said they were very much feminists while 47% more described themselves as somewhat feminist.

Eighty-five percent of the respondents felt that abortion should be allowed for reasons other than rape or incest. Only 7% believed that abortion should never be permitted. Fifty-eight percent believe that abortion should be allowed just because "a woman has a right to her own body." Interestingly, of the 88 Catholics in the group, only 21% believe that women should not have an abortion under any conditions. On the other hand, 34% felt that women should make decisions about their own bodies, including the decision to abort. Ten percent of the 163 Protestants opposed abortion, and another 12% believe abortion should occur only in cases of rape or incest. The remaining number, for whatever reasons, were not opposed to abortion.

While only 7% believe sexual activity should take place only within marriage, another 15% believe that people should have intercourse only when "in love." Eighty-seven percent feel that there are many reasons for sexual intercourse between consenting people, including fun. We asked if our respondents hoped for or expected to have sex with someone other than their usual partner at the con, and about 27% answered affirmatively. Sixty-two percent did not think extramarital sexual activity was immoral. However, 90% of respondents who answered the question "how many intimate encounters have you participated in at this con" replied "none." The sexual picture, then, is one of liberal thinking and non-judgmental attitudes, some wishful thinking, and not a lot of actuality.

Most fen do not smoke (81%) and 41% object very much to others smoking around them. Another 36% object to some degree. Of course, some of these object only because smoke makes them sick, not as a moral issue. Twenty-three percent do not drink alcohol at all, and another 70% say they drink only moderately (however they may have defined moderately).

Twenty-seven percent use other mind- or emotion-altering substances. This is indicative of the rather moderate lifestyle of fen, we believe, and belies images some people have of them.

Most people say they come to conventions primarily for fun (78%), and nearly half say they come to meet old friends or to communicate with people who have the same interests. Many come for business, such as huckstering, but we believe that many hucksters huckster in order to afford to come to conventions. About one fourth of respondents come to conventions to meet authors and a third come primarily to attend meetings. A few (16%) come primarily for "philosophical reasons"--to consider where they are in their lives, to discuss issues such as ecology or the destruction of the earth, or, we believe, to share dreams about the future. And 25% list as primary reason for attending simply to escape from reality, or to get away from the mundane chores, values, and problems that constitute the bulk of their lives. Most only come to about three cons per year, but would come to more if they could afford it.

Most fen believe that fandom is very different from mundane culture. Respondents see other fen as more liberal and open than mundanes, non-judgmental and accepting of others--along with being a little deviant, very playful, and so on. They are caring, friendly, and gentle, having a sense of community. Fen also say that they are misfits and loners--about 49% describe themselves as loners or not having many friends while in school, while another 41% say they had only a few friends in school. Sixty-two percent are either only children or oldest children. Finally, they note that fen are more intelligent and literate than people in the mundane world. are curious and aware and have a great concern for the future of humankind. Our own observations of fen substantiate this. They are individualistic and non-judgmental but very caring and gentle people of high intelligence. One feels very safe and secure at cons, even amid a couple of hundred relative strangers, many in weird garb.

Fen as a group are highly creative. Thirty-nine percent have written science fiction and 10% of these have published their work, while 24% write non-science fiction with 11% of these having published. About 24% write poetry, 12% compose music, 7% sculpt, and 26% are artists. Altogether, only about 30% say that they engage in no artistic effort at all.

****

The fen who answered our questionnaire very often argued back at us--about the questions, about the format, about the validity of the research, and about our intelligence and nosiness. Some were moderate and understanding--

> "Excuse me, but no matter how many responses you receive, I hope that when you summarize the material . . . you understand that owing to the form and type of items, the statistical validity is limited."

Others were not so nice--

> "Dammit, whoever wrote this survey should be fileted. Be more specific in your questions and don't ask such patently stupid ones. Do you know anything about SF or Fandom? Know your topic, you JERK!"

Many did not like the ambiguity of questions which were intended to be respondent-definitive. "The questions are poorly written, ambiguous, the responses are not mutually exclusive or not comprehensive," "categories offered usually were pigeonholes that are about as appropriate as census forms," "distinctly fuzzy and need more definition," "could not be answered accurately within the choices given, so I made my own choices." And

> Being an aspiring academic myself, I find many questions in the questionnaire too nebulous. I am quite sure the results from this survey will be misleading. The assumptions made in some of these questions seem to indicate that the researchers of this project already have certain unfounded conclusions about SF fandom. If this comment sounds vague, now you know how I feel about a great deal of the questions. Don't give me a bad reputation in SF fandom. However, I do appreciate your efforts in treating aspects of science fiction seriously.

The final blow--one refused to grant us our Ph.D.'s for the research. Some, however, liked the survey, saying that it had more relevant questions about "who I am than any other I've answered," liking the ability to answer back and to add comments, and so on. Many thanked us, warmly, for our interest in finding their "true selves" and in our interest in fandom.

Some, of course, warned us "A con is not a good place to ask such a questionnaire. Fen are usually not prone to take such things seriously. I do not." And

> "Warning: questionnaires can become very ineffective if not entirely useless in the hands of fen. Why don'tcha just come to a few cons yourself, huh? That's what Margaret Mead would have done."

Some asked "Why do you folks want to know this stuff which is essentially none of your business? Do I detect a 'moral majority' backlash?" and "What is all this nosyness for anywho?" Still, they did answer the questions, and there were many "thank you's" and "good luck's."

We had asked some fairly pointed questions about sexual activity and other "morality" issues, as much to belie the image of fen as a bunch of freako-weirdies as anything. Many fen were very offended by those questions. They said that these were "none of your damn business," "you emphasize sex too much," "I prefer not to answer [the sex questions]. I consider [them] quite morally offensive." Some were sure we had already categorized fen--"we're all atheist-pagan loose men and women who touch everyone we see and are rampantly liberal . . . ," "your survey is slanted toward the view that fen are drug-crazed homosexual/nymphomaniacal witches;" and one ran her/his own survey: "Do sociologists

. . . prefer A. single sex, B. Quad, C. Gang bangs . . . since they're obviously obsessed with the subject." One astute fan observed that "Sexual mores seem to be the same as many other conventions. However, SF fandom likes to dress in costume . . . and to spook the mundane."

Another criticism was that the survey seemed to lump science fiction fandom and Society for Creative Anachronism together. While there is much overlap, some people are a little touchy on the subject. "I deplore the kind of fandom stemming from "crushes" on personae. I feel these people are really out of touch with reality. It gives SF a bad name." One fan put the issue into perspective, saying:

> You shouldn't try to lump SCA and fandom together as a group. While there has been a lot more crossover in recent years, most SCA members still consider fans to be mundanes and most or at least a lot of fans rank SCA people below mundanes. I've never understood this except that fans do tend, in some cases, to have an elitist view of themselves.

We believe that many did indeed take the survey seriously, and were interested in it. Specific items in the questionnaire commented on most frequently were ones on witchcraft, sex, personae, and some of the "quick and dirty" social issues such as feminism, abortion, homosexuality, and welfare. These last, we should note, were not well phrased nor "scientific." They were meant as much to elicit immediate reactions as answers, and they surely did that. Many people were appalled that we thought fen might believe in or practice witchcraft. Many were delighted. Homosexuality called out much comment. While we found very few people who verified their homosexuality, many were pleased that we recognized this lifestyle in our questions. Some people accused us of thinking all fen were gay; on the other hand, at least one felt that we should have recognized gay marriages. Abortion was hardly an issue. Fen in general felt that, even though they might not choose abortion for themselves, (or homosexuality, or marrying outside one's race or religion, etc.), others had a right to choose what was best for them.

Fen answered or commented widely on themselves and others as fen. The consensus seemed to be that fen are "a little strange, maybe, but that's a [positive] attribute."

> I feel that most people who attend SF or Wargame cons have the advantage of stepping out of the 'real world' with company. Readers of other escapist fiction never extend their daydreams beyond their minds . . .

"SF cons can be both more serious and more crazy than normal conventions . . ."

> most of them believe in abortion . . . population control, space exploration to keep earth livable, which leads to ecology, solar, wind, and nuclear power, etc. The people involved seem to support each other more than in the 'outside' world . . . fen will call coast to coast to share joy or commiseration . . . Perhaps a fair analogy

would be pioneers who settled the west--distinctively individualistic, wanting both distance and neighbors, they helped one another and they shaped their own future.

"It's so sad to go back to the mundane world after so much openness and friendliness. (Post-con triste.) However, one can overload on too much closeness with unfamiliar people."
On fandom as a sub-culture, a fan said

> I feel that your wording, which tends to portray fans as a sub-culture, or a group of individuals who are substantially different from a "mundane" world, is off-base. The conventions vary only due to party spirit and mood of participants. If you are only "different" 2 or 3 weekends a year, you can only be considered different 0.3% of the time. . . .

We disagree with this comment, because we feel that cons are only the outward expression of fen way of life. Fen take their ideals, hopes, and dreams back to the real world with them the rest of the year. At the other extreme, a fan says "I question this whole thing of SF/SCA/etc. as un-reality. What we are (I think) evolving is an alternate society to mundane mainstream culture. . . ."

David Loye has given a social-psychological interpretation to people who are somewhat deviant from mainstream society because of anomie or alienation. Anomie is characteristic of the conservatively-raised person who depends on clear-cut rules of society, and anomie arises from " . . . the feeling that there is not enough coherent shape in the social environment for the individual to be able to find a place, a goal, or a style or life that receives any social support." Such a person becomes anomic when the standards of society are in flux.

On the other hand, alienation has to do with the liberally-raised person, nourished in a family which

> . . . encourages independent action and experimentation and is primarily growth oriented. The child is consistently rewarded for behavior that shows development of initiative; life is seen as a process, and progress is a prime value. In times of social change, where innovation frequently appears called for, persons of this type become impatient with what they perceive as outmoded elements of the culture and succumb to alienation from the "system." If their alienation is not too great and they have access to movements within the religious institution they may become advocates of ecclesiastic reform. . . if they are more alienated from the religious institution but still recognize personal religious needs, they may opt for one of the cultic religious forms. . . .[5]

Fen are not anomic. They know who they are, are mostly pleased about being individuals, and make individualism a central aspect of their belief. Rather, our study indicates that fen are, to a greater or lesser degree, a group of alienated people; and they have turned to fandom almost as a religion, or what we deem a "paracult." Berger says about alienation that " . . . the structures of the society are experienced not as human creations or projections of the self, but as external and alien forces impinging on the development of the self."[6] Fen find the pressures to conformity from whatever source an impingement on their persons, and life in the United States an inauthentic and sometimes insane way of approaching the future. For some fen, only reading science fiction to escape today's world is enough. Others congregate in communal groups at cons, seeking people who are visionaries like themselves in what is almost a form of cult, an activity which is characterized by common beliefs about the sacred and the supernatural, common values shared among members, who practice common rituals, and have a sense of community.[7]

A large number, in fact, eschew patriarchal religion and have returned to old ways of belief. In many senses, fandom is religious in nature. Hargrove says that

> The search for meaning extends to infinity. As a result, we generally live in three worlds at once: the world of nature . . . the everyday world made of the pattern in which we have come to understand our existence; and an ideal world created by our extension of that pattern for everyday reality.[8]

Fen have extended their ideal world into one which is shared by other fen, into

> . . . some kind of community--some group of people who share the activities and anticipations of the religion, even if they may not practice it together with any amount of frequency or regularity.[9]

Although much of what happens at science fiction conventions is fun, that fun is for release in the safe extended family-type gatherings of cons. Underlying all the fun is a security for fen know they will not be judged deviant in this society, can speak to others about their visions, and can share the hopes they have for a better world.

Our respondents are highly creative, highly individualistic, somewhat deviant, with a view of the future that decries present-day structures. They are highly intelligent but are not in positions to gain them much wealth. Many are only children or oldest children, on whom demands for conformity were discouraged. They are really quite moral in their behavior, but do not condemn others for any kind of lifestyle which may be their choice. One might believe that, to avoid what they consider the insanity of today's world, they pull into dreamworlds. That may be true, but only to a very limited extent. They attend conventions to get another dose of reality, as it were; and they go back into mundanity with their ideals, dreams, and capabilities to be used in service of their visions. They find at conventions not only relief but a validation of their beliefs.

Of course we, the authors, identify ourselves as fen, and therefore may not be entirely objective. We believe we are, perhaps, a conclave of people who are a part of what Marilyn

Ferguson has termed the "Aquarian Conspiracy."[10] Certainly we would agree with the following respondent in characterizing fen and fandom.

> I believe SF fandom is a very special group of vibrant, thinking, individuals. Within our group we may bare our souls share our deepest longings, and strive to make tomorrow as beautiful as possible. We may seem like dreamers and silly children (no matter what our age may be) to others, but our dreams will come true. For enough of us believe in the future of man to be willing to do whatever is necessary to insure the stars and beyond for our children.

Purdue University

Notes

[1] The Science Fiction Encyclopedia, ed. Peter Nicholls (Garden City, New York: Dolphin Books, 1979), p. 206.

[2] Ibid.

[3] Johnathan H. Turner. Sociology: Studying the Human System. (Santa Monica, California: Goodyear Publishing Co., 1981).

[4] Barbara Hargrove. The Sociology of Religion. (Arlington Heights, Ill.: AHM Publishing Corp., 1979), p. 77.

[5] Ibid., p. 289.

[6] Turner, p. 360.

[7] Peter L. Berger. The Sacred Canopy. (Garden City, N.Y.: Doubleday, 1967), ch. 4.

[8] Hargrove, p. 6.

[9] Emile Durkheim, quoted in Hargrove, p. 8.

[10] Marilyn Ferguson. The Aquarian Conspiracy. (Los Angeles, CA: J. P. Tarcher, Inc., 1980).

Appendix

FRIDAY, SEPTEMBER 3

1:00 - 2:00 p.m.	--	THE STATE OF THE ART IN SCHOLARSHIP AND CRITICISM (Session 1)
Chairperson:		Gary K. Wolfe, Roosevelt University
Discussants:		Thomas D. Clareson, The College of Wooster
		Arthur O. Lewis, Jr., The Pennsylvania State University
		Joe De Bolt, Central Michigan University
		James Gunn, The University of Kansas
2:15 - 4:00 p.m.	--	IS THERE A THEORY OF FANTASY? (Session II)
Chairperson:		Catherine L. McClenahan, Marquette University
Paper:		"Fantasy and the Believing Reader" by Orson Scott Card, Notre Dame University
Paper:		"Stephen King: Fantasist or SF Writer?" by Joseph Patrouch, Jr., The University of Dayton
Discussants:		Tom Moylan, The University of Wisconsin--Waukesha
		Gary K. Wolfe, Roosevelt University
		Algis Budrys, Chicago
4:15 - 6:00 p.m.	--	WOMEN IN SCIENCE FICTION (Session III)
Chairperson:		Roger C. Schlobin, North Central Campus of Purdue University
Paper:		"The Days of Future Past: Future Nostalgia in Lessing and LeGuin" by Kathe Davis Finney, Kent State University
Paper:		"Science Fiction's Philosophical Women" by Richard Law, Kutztown State College
Paper:		"Woman on the Edge of Narrative: Cultural Stories in Marge Piercy's Utopia" by David L. Foster, The University of Colorado
Paper:		"Women at Work In/On the Future" by Janice M. Bogstad, The University of Wisconsin
Discussants:		Marleen Barr, Virginia Polytechnic Institute and State University
		Mary T. Brizzi, Trumbull Campus of Kent State University

SATURDAY, SEPTEMBER 4

2:00 - 3:00 p.m.	--	THE MECHANICAL GOD (Session IV)
Chairperson:		Marshall B. Tymn, Eastern Michigan University
Discussants:		Thomas P. Dunn, Hamilton Campus of Miami University
		Richard D. Erlich, Miami University
		Donald M. Hassler, Kent State University
3:15 - 4:30 p.m.	--	DEATH AND THE SERPENT (Session V)
Chairperson:		Marshall B. Tymn, Eastern Michigan University
Paper:		"Immortality in Roger Zelazny" by Joseph Sanders, Lakeland Community College
Paper:		"Deathless Humans in Horror Fiction" by Sam H. Vasbinder, The University of Akron
Paper:		"Jack Vance's *To Live Forever*" by Gregory M. Shreve, Geauga Campus of Kent State University
Paper:		"Lovecraft and *The Dunwich Horror*" by John McInnis, Northeast Louisiana University
Paper:		"Immortality and Transcendence in the Fiction of James Tiptree, Jr." by Mark Siegel, The University of Wyoming
4:40 - 6:00 p.m.	--	FANS AND THE FUTURE (Session VI)
Chairperson:		Elizabeth Anne Hull, William Rainey Harper College
Paper:		"Science Fiction Fans: A Study of Enthusiasm and Endeavor" by Beverly Friend, Oakton Community College
Paper:		"Freaking the Mundane: A Sociological Look at Science Fiction Conventions, and Vice Versa" by Phyllis J. Day and Nora G. Day, Purdue University
Paper:		"Science Fiction and Human Survival" by C. A. Hilgartner, M.D., Rochester
Paper:		"History of the Mobius Theater Group" by Jane Bloomquist and William McMillan, Northwestern University

SUNDAY, SEPTEMBER 5

1:00 - 2:00 p.m.	--	STUDIES OF JAMES BLISH (Session VII)
Chairperson:		Janice M. Bogstad, The University of Wisconsin
Paper:		"Biographic and Bibliographic Work on Blish" by Philip E. Kaveny, The University of Wisconsin
Paper:		"Community in *Cities in Flight* and *The Seedling Stars*" by Janice M. Bogstad
Paper:		"The City in Blish's Trilogy *After Such Knowledge*" by Jared Lobdell, Carnegie Mellon University

Appendix

2:15 - 4:30 p.m.	--	PAPERS ON CLARKE, ELLISON, DELANY AND OTHERS (Session VIII) [including two additional women writers if not time to treat them on Friday]
Chairperson:		Elizabeth Anne Hull, William Rainey Harper College
Paper:		"Clarke's The Fountains of Paradise and the Future" by Tor H. Thorsen, Boyce Community College
Paper:		"Harlan Ellison's Use of the Narrator's Voice" by Joseph Patrouch, Jr., The University of Dayton
Paper:		"Ellison's Fiction" by Evelina Smith, Trumbull Campus of Kent State University
Paper:		"Coma and Brain: The Clockwork World of Robin Cook" by Thomas P. Dunn, Hamilton Campus of Miami University
Paper:		"Moon-Watcher, Man, and Star-Child: 2001 as Paradigm" by Richard D. Erlich, Miami University
Paper:		"The Racial Grammar of Bellona: Ethnicity, Language and Meaning in Samuel R. Delany's Dhalgren" by Marleen Barr, Virginia Polytechnic Institute and State University
Paper:		"A Further Look at Anne McCaffrey" by Mary T. Brizzi, Trumbull Campus of Kent State University
Paper:		"Study of Kate Wilhelm" by Jim Villani, Youngstown State University
4:45 - 6:00 p.m.	--	WRITERS YOU MAY NOT HAVE HEARD OF: BIBLIOGRAPHIC SURVEY (Session IX)
Chairperson:		Barbara Emrys, Columbia College of De Paul University
Paper:		"Women Publishing Women: F & SF in the Feminist Press" by Barbara Emrys
Paper:		"Intersections and Influences: Post-Forties F & SF Through the Mainstream" by Karen Axness, The University of Wisconsin
Paper:		"New Writers Meet the Aliens" by Tom Porter, The University of Wisconsin
Paper:		"Notable Newcomers to Young Adult F & SF" by Beverly DeWeese, Milwaukee Public Libraries

www.ingramcontent.com/pod-product-compliance
Lightning Source LLC
LaVergne TN
LVHW041632070426
835507LV00008B/570